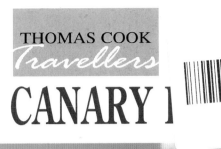

THOMAS COOK
Travellers

CANARY I

C000060511

BY
PAUL MURPHY

Produced by AA Publishing

Written by Paul Murphy

Original photography by Clive Sawyer

Edited, designed and produced by AA Publishing.
© The Automobile Association 1995.
Maps © The Automobile Association 1995.
Reprinted 1997; February and July 1998.

Distributed in the United Kingdom by AA Publishing, Norfolk
House, Priestley Road, Basingstoke, Hampshire RG24 9NY.

A CIP catalogue record for this book is available from the
British Library.

ISBN 0 7495 1012 9

All rights reserved. No part of this publication may be reproduced,
stored in a retrieval system, or transmitted in any form or by any means
– electronic, photocopying, recording, or otherwise – unless the written
permission of the publishers has been obtained beforehand.
This book may not be lent, resold, hired out or otherwise disposed of by
way of trade in any form of binding or cover other than that in which it is
published, without the prior consent of the publisher.

The contents of this publication are believed correct at the time of
printing. Nevertheless, the publishers cannot accept responsibility for
any errors or omissions, or for changes in the details given in this guide
or for the consequences of any reliance on the information provided by
the same. Assessments of attractions, hotels, restaurants and so forth are
based upon the author's own experience and therefore descriptions given
in this guide necessarily contain an element of subjective opinion which
may not reflect the publisher's opinion or dictate a reader's own
experiences on another occasion.
**We have tried to ensure accuracy in this guide, but things do
change and we would be grateful if readers would advise us of any
inaccuracies they may encounter.**

Published by AA Publishing (a trading name of Automobile Association
Developments Limited, whose registered office is Norfolk House,
Priestley Road, Basingstoke, Hampshire RG24 9NY. Registered number
1878835) and the Thomas Cook Group Ltd.

Colour separation: BTB Colour Reproduction, Whitchurch, Hampshire.

Printed by: Edicoes ASA, Oporto, Portugal.

Title page: *view of Graciosa Island*
Above: *Puerto de la Cruz*

Contents

About this Book

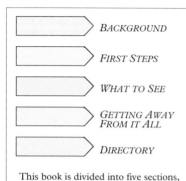

BACKGROUND

FIRST STEPS

WHAT TO SEE

GETTING AWAY FROM IT ALL

DIRECTORY

This book is divided into five sections, identified by the above colour coding.

Background gives an introduction to the islands – their history, geography, politics and culture.

First Steps offers practical advice on arriving and getting around.

What to See is an alphabetical listing of places to visit, interspersed with walks and drives.

Getting Away From it All highlights places off the beaten track where it is possible to relax and enjoy peace and quiet.

Finally, the **Directory** provides practical information – from shopping and entertainment to children and sport, including a section on business matters. Special highly illustrated *features* on specific aspects of the islands appear throughout the book.

Fishing boats, El Cortillo

BACKGROUND

These islands enjoy a fortunate climate...they offer not only a good rich soil...but also wild fruits to nourish people without work or effort...these are the Elysian Fields of which Homer sang.

PLUTARCH
Life of Sertorius 1st–2nd century AD

Introduction

*T*he Canary Islands were born as an international holiday playground in the late 1950s. Since then they have entered the north European psyche as a synonym for winter sunshine, and today the islands welcome over six million tourists each year.

Despite its popularity, however, few people have any real knowledge of the archipelago. Even naming the seven islands, beyond Gran Canaria, Tenerife and Lanzarote, would be irksome to most. The Canaries are popular precisely because they provide great numbers of people with simple 'sun and fun' holidays, and this has led to some resorts being transformed into concrete jungles and pastiches of home-life culture. Yet to typecast the whole of a diverse island group on the evidence of two or three of its resorts is as ridiculous as writing off all Spain for a deviant *costa* or two.

Beyond the beaches there is much to be commended by even the sternest travel critic. The scenery on all these volcanic islands is spectacular: from soft green, wooded valleys to charred and still-smoking lunarscapes, from Arizona-like gorges to snowy peaks and Sahara-scale sand dunes. Four out of the ten Spanish National Parks are concentrated in this relatively tiny archipelago, giving the lie to anyone who believes nature always comes second to tourism here.

Cultural, historical and ethnic features are admittedly limited, but there is more than enough to occupy the

CANARY ISLANDS

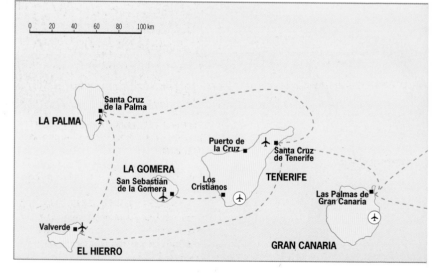

LOCATOR

average two-week stay. Caves of the original aboriginal inhabitants lie open to discovery, the cities have fine museums and galleries, and there are superb examples of Spanish Colonial architecture in towns untouched by tourism. Folk traditions and island heritage are also still

The wide sweep of Playa de las Teresitas, with Tenerife's capital, Santa Cruz, sprawling behind the headland

very much alive – to see *Canarios* at their best, just catch a fiesta.

It's quite easy to sample the 'real' Canaries. Just get off the beach, drive away from the resorts and look around you. You'll be surprised at what lies beyond.

History

1st–2nd century BC

The Canaries are settled by a tribe with both Cro-Magnon and Mediterranean features, probably of Berber origin from North Africa and subsequently called Guanches (see pages 10–11).

25BC–AD23

Ships arrive from the Roman colony of Mauritania, find native dogs and name the islands (see page 24).

1st–2nd century AD

The Roman writer, Pliny the Elder, mentions the islands for the first time in his *Natural History*. The islands are mapped by the Greek geographer, Ptolemy, who recognises El Hierro as the westernmost point of the known world.

Around 1312

Genoese seafarer, Lanzalotto Malocello, lands on the island of Tytheroygatra. His motives and actions are unclear, but the island is later renamed Lanzarote.

1339–42

The first mention of Isla Canaria appears on maps. Spanish vessels are launched in search of the islands, though no conquests are recorded.

Late 14th–early 15th centuries

The Canaries come increasingly to the notice of European slave-traders and treasure-hunters. In 1402 the Norman baron, Jean de Béthencourt with the help of Spanish nobleman Gadifer de la Salle, sails under the flag of Henry II of Castile, intending to capture Gran Canaria and Tenerife. Instead he occupies Lanzarote and begins colonisation.

1404–06

Using Lanzarote as a staging post for reinforcements, Béthencourt sails to Fuerteventura and within a year, succeeds in subduing the island. He then turns his attentions to El Hierro, where he tricks the small population into slavery. However, he meets strong armed resistance on La Gomera, Gran Canaria and La Palma and returns to France.

1478–88

Ferdinand and Isabella of Spain order the second phase of the Conquest. A force led by Juan Réjon lands on Gran Canaria and founds Las Palmas. After five years of bitter fighting Gran Canaria is captured. After another five years La Gomera is also subdued.

1492

Christopher Columbus uses the islands as a final staging post before his voyage to the New World (see pages 36–7).

1493

Alonso Fernández de Lugo lands on La Palma and completes its capture by stealth, tricking the last resisting chieftain into captivity.

1494

De Lugo's forces on Tenerife are routed in the Orotava Valley. But de Lugo returns to the valley with reinforcements and, following a bloody battle, the site is proclaimed La Victoria (Victory) in honour of the last battle of the Conquest.

16th–17th century

The islands use slave labour to gain economic wealth, first from sugar, then from wine.

Early 19th century

Cochineal, a red dye extracted from cactus-feeding insects, becomes the new island industry. This lasts until the advent of chemical dyes elsewhere in the world in the 1870s. Its collapse leads to large-scale emigration to South America.

1852

In order to stimulate the Canarian

The Guanches' sacred Roque Nublo above Tejeda on Gran Canaria

economy, Santa Cruz de Tenerife and Las Palmas de Gran Canaria are declared free-trade zones by Queen Isabella II. They soon become two of the busiest ports in the world.

1880s
The first Canarian bananas are exported and become a mainstay of the islands' economy.

1936
General Francisco Franco, mistrusted by the Spanish government, is posted to Tenerife. Here he meets fellow conspirators to plan the military coup which will lead to the Spanish Civil War (1936–9).

The islands quickly fall to his forces.

1960s
Tenerife and Gran Canaria embrace package tourism.

1971
The most recent volcanic eruption on the islands occurs on La Palma.

1982
The Canaries are made an autonomous region under the new post-Franco constitution.

1989
The Canary Islands, as part of Spain, are accepted as full members of the European Community.

THE GUANCHES

The term 'Guanche' meant 'native of Tenerife' in the original island language, but was subsequently used as a name for all the islanders who occupied the archipelago before the Spanish Conquest in the 15th century.

The Guanches almost certainly came from North Africa in the 1st or 2nd century BC, possibly fleeing persecution, possibly in primitive boats. Little is known about their origins, and new theories and discoveries are frequently advanced. In appearance they were fair-skinned and sometimes blue-eyed and blond-haired (the Arabs did not colonise North Africa until much later).

There are no written records of the Guanches until the medieval voyages of Malocello and the Spanish *conquistadores* (see pages 8–9). The Spanish discovered a people still living in the Stone Age: metals were unknown to them, and many Guanches still lived in caves, both natural and man-made. They were by no means savages, however. Some of the earliest Spanish journals praise them highly for their morality, courage and intelligence.

The best indicators of Guanche life have been found in their tombs. Like the ancient Egyptians, they ritually embalmed their dead, and mummies and other finds are on display at the archaeological museums in Santa Cruz de Tenerife and Las Palmas de Gran Canaria. They also appear to have had a cryptic language of symbols, which have been found carved on rocks. So few of these have survived, however, that translation is extremely difficult.

Reminders of a lost culture – statues of
the Guanche people at Candelaria,
Tenerife, and Doramas Park, Las Palmas,
Gran Canaria

When the Spanish arrived
most islands were divided into
several chiefdoms or kingdoms
(*Menceyatos*), each ruled by a
mencey who was advised by a
council of elderly men. As
elsewhere in the New World, the
Spanish pursued a policy of divide and
rule, making alliances with friendly
kings and encouraging Guanche to fight
Guanche, until resistance was quelled.
Aside from set-piece battles, however,
the body count on both sides appears
to have been relatively low and the
inadvertent import of European
diseases probably killed more Guanches
than battle.

Life on the post-conquest islands
varied. Many Guanches were enslaved;
collaborators were well treated; a
minority inter-married, and many were
simply ignored by the new colonists. A
significant number remained in hiding
in the
mountains, but
many
Guanches
were coerced
and
intimidated by
the Spanish
Inquisition into
'abandoning
their roots.

Within a
few decades it is estimated that two-
thirds of the indigenous people had
disappeared in one form or another and
within a century or so this ancient
society had all but vanished.

Geography

*T*he Canary Islands comprise seven major and six very small islands, situated between 96km and 304km off the northwest coast of North Africa. Some 496km lie between the easternmost island (Fuerteventura) and the westernmost island (El Hierro). The next stop west of El Hierro is the Americas.

For historical reasons the Canaries are Spanish territory although the southern coast of Spain lies 1,120km to the north. Geographically, the Canaries actually belong to a larger island grouping, known as Macaronesia (Blessed Islands), which comprises the Azores, Madeira and Cape Verde islands. All of these volcanic islands have topographical and fauna and flora features in common.

Landscapes and statistics
Each island is of volcanic origin and is dotted with volcanic cones, either long extinct and overgrown, or quite bare and, on Lanzarote and La Palma, still smouldering (see pages 14–15).

The largest of the islands is Tenerife with an area of 2,057 sq km and a population of 600,000. It is dominated by Mount Teide, at 3,718m the highest mountain in all of Spanish territory. The island's mountainous northeast and

northwest corners are lush, its southern shores parched and arid.

The next largest island is Fuerteventura, with an area of 1,731 sq km. With a population of just 30,000, however, this is the emptiest of the islands. Fuerteventura is also the oldest and, topographically, the least dramatic island, many of its volcanoes reduced to mere hummocks by the erosion of 20 million years. It is almost completely barren.

Gran Canaria covers a similar size area to Fuerteventura of 1,532 sq km, and has the highest and most densely packed population (nearly 700,000) of any of the islands, two-thirds of whom live in Las Palmas. Gran Canaria is a classic volcanic cone in profile with a series of mountains climbing towards a central peak of 1,949m (Pico de las Nieves). The north of the island is wetter and cooler than the arid south and here the vegetation is at its greenest.

Lanzarote and La Palma are similar in both size – 795 sq km and 728 sq km respectively – and population (54,000 and 80,000). The south of Lanzarote is also very dry. It was devastated by 18th-century eruptions which have left a fantastic, lunar-like landscape. The north is comparatively green and mountainous.

La Palma has a great central ridge (*cumbre*) of aligned mountains running north–south along its length, culminating

Striated rock formations at Los Gigantes, Tenerife

Volcanic Mount Teide seen from Las Rosas, La Gomera

in a massive mature crater or *caldera* (see pages 14–15). This is by far the greenest of all the islands and the only place (aside from Tenerife's Barranco del Infierno) where running water can regularly be found.

La Gomera is around half the size of Lanzarote and La Palma at 378 sq km, and is inhabited by just 20,000 people. La Gomera, like Gran Canaria, is a dome-shaped island and also has a north–south weather divide. At the centre is a lush plateau, almost continually covered in mist, home to a dense laurel forest.

Last and least is El Hierro, covering 277 sq km with a population of just 7,400. El Hierro is a semi-circular sweeping curve of an island. Were the sea to be rolled back and the circle completed, a huge collapsed volcanic crater would be revealed. The landscape is green and varied, though not as dramatic as the other western islands. (For details of the six tiny islets off Lanzarote and Fuerteventura see pages 136–7.)

VOLCANOES

All the Canaries are volcanic islands, typically formed when molten rock and ash force their way up through the earth's core and the seabed to form a cone-shaped island, often scored by deep gullies (*barrancos*).

The first to be born was Fuerteventura, some 20 million years ago; Lanzarote appeared about 4 million years later, followed by Gran Canaria after another 2 to 3 million years. The rest of the group emerged over the course of the next 13 million years.

The nature of the volcanic scenery on each island depends how recent and how extensive the eruptions were, and on the forces of erosion and nature's reclamation of the land. There are few places in the world as spectacular as the fantastic 'moonscapes' of Tenerife and Lanzarote (only Hawaii and Iceland are comparable). Here, cataclysmic forces occurred very recently in geographical terms.

Mount Teide was blowing as Columbus passed in 1492 and there were further sizeable eruptions in 1604, 1605, 1704–5, 1706, 1798 and 1909. The south of Lanzarote was devastated between 1730 and 1736 and suffered again from 1812 to 1824. The most recent eruptions occurred on La Palma,

in 1949 and 1971. These were slight compared to earlier occasions; the explosion that formed the island's Caldera de Taburiente, some 400,000 years ago, was enormous – it is from here that the word *caldera* (volcanic crater) originates.

As you tour the *malpais* (badlands) caused by the eruptions you can see the three main types of volcanic debris: *picon*, or *lapilli*, the tiny, light cinder particles put to good effect by Canarian farmers (see pages 72–3); pumice, or *escoria*, small, lightweight honeycombed rocks produced by the formation of gas bubbles in slow-flowing lava; and volcanic 'bombs'. heavy solid rocks, sometimes as big as footballs, with a brittle outer coat.

The lava, too, comes in distinct

The most spectacular 'badlands' are to be found on Tenerife (far left and below) and Lanzarote (left and below)

types. If it is the fast-flowing variety it cools into rope-like coils and is known as *pahoe-pahoe* (the Hawaiian term for rope lava). The slower moving debris, which cools into slab-like folds, is known as pillow lava.

Geologists will have a field day wandering the Cañadas del Teide (see pages 88–9) identifying the various volcanic rock types. But if you simply want to be entertained, see how Lanzarote designer César Manrique made both a home and tourist attractions from the underground passages formed by the molten lava, and visit the Cueva de los Verdes on Lanzarote. Above all don't miss a trip to Lanzarote's Montañas del Fuego, first by coach, then by foot (see pages 68–9 and 78–9).

Culture

*T*he Canary Islands are a pot-pourri of many different cultures. On the larger islands you will find field workers and resort workers, cave-dwellers and city-dwellers, all within a few kilometres of each other. Yet many Canarios have never even left their islands, and the difference between Las Palmas and El Hierro is mind-boggling. What, then, is the cultural bond (if indeed, there is such a thing) that holds this fragmented society together?

Guanche culture

The Guanche language, dress, religion and other habits were extinguished by the *conquistadores* long ago (see pages 10–11). Judging by the poor state of repair that Guanche sites are found in today, modern Canarios seem to have no great interest in their ancestors. This apparent lack of interest may partly be due to the absence of information about the first islanders, which makes it almost impossible to draw up a true picture of their society. There are still cave-dwellers today (at Chinamada on Tenerife, for example), but they probably have virtually nothing in common with their forebears.

Spanish culture

The islanders may speak Spanish and look Spanish but does this make them Spanish? A Las Palmas banker may say yes, a Lanzarote farmer may say no. For many years, particularly under the Franco regime, the islands were 'forgotten Spain' (as were many mainland rural regions). This feeling of 'poor relations' was graphically illustrated, until quite recently, by the fact that Canarian TV screens would go blank during Spanish television commercial breaks; advertisers simply didn't think it was worth showing their products to the impoverished islanders. The new wealth of tourism has changed that way of thinking.

Canarian separatism is often mooted and is the subject of popular graffiti, but true independence (as opposed to

A quiet moment in the pretty village of Fataga (Gran Canaria)

autonomy, which the islands do enjoy) is not really on the agenda. That situation is accepted quite happily by the Canarian banana-growers, who sell over 90 per cent of their crop to mainland Spain.

The popular images of Spanish culture, such as bullfighting and flamenco dancing, mean nothing to Canarios (the latter is staged only for tourists). Spanish *joie de vivre* at fiesta time is well embraced, however, and the Carnival celebrations on Tenerife are said to be the best outside Rio de Janeiro and New Orleans. This is also a chance for the island's South American cultural influence to emerge (see pages 8–9). Café life (see pages 164–5), the siesta and football fervour are other shared Spanish passions.

Inter-island rivalry

The two capitals of Las Palmas and Santa Cruz de Tenerife are forever competing to offer the best banks, the best port, the best cultural facilities and so on. For example, Las Palmas recently won a fierce battle for a second Canarian University to compete with that of La Laguna on Tenerife. The other islands are regarded as backwaters and La Gomera, in particular, is frequently the butt of jokes.

New influences

Tourism has inevitably had a major effect on many islanders. While those with businesses in the new resorts of Playa de Las Américas and Maspalomas have prospered and become the *nouveau riches*, many more islanders have been left behind. Youngsters have swapped a life of drudgery in the fields for low wages in foreign-owned hotel thralldom while their communities, starved of new blood, slowly die. This is surely the worst

Tenerife costume, here modelled by folk dancers, echoes the vivid island flora

of both worlds. Others, keen to develop their own communities for the tourist *peseta*, are either knowingly or unwittingly bulldozing their own heritage. Conservationists, such as César Manrique on Lanzarote, are seeking to redress this balance and re-educate the people, and moreover has proved that it is possible to combine local pride, character and integrity with profitable tourism. These are exciting times for the Canarios. Money and adventure beckon, but family roots and village loyalties are still strong.

TOURISM

The adverse effects of tourism on the southern coastlines of Gran Canaria and Tenerife are well documented and well discussed. But this does not necessarily mean that lessons have been learned. In fact the large-scale developments of Jandía on Fuerteventura and the ridiculously overcrowded bay of Puerto Rico on Gran Canaria argue the reverse. Only Lanzarote and La Palma enforce meaningful controls on tourism development (no advertising hoardings, no high-rise hotels etc).

There are of course many benefits to the islands and its visitors from the careful development of tourism. The debate goes something like this:

For large-scale development: new roads, hotels and apartments bring more jobs for the locals (Canarian unemployment is very high); new roads attract visitors to villages so craft, souvenir and restaurant premises can thrive; work in tourism is all year round and not subject to the hardship or vicissitudes of farming.

Against large-scale development: hoteliers and time-share operators bring in their own staff and exclude the locals; as young people leave their villages for tourism work, so these settlements are depopulated and die (this in itself is arguably a bad thing, but commercially it is also folly as villages also attract tourists); tourists swamp villages and irrevocably change their character; pollution and destruction of flora and fauna.

A related issue is the direction which tourism should take in the Canaries. Do visitors really want to suffer constant haranguing from time-share touts, or see signs saying 'No Spanish Food here'? The 'pile it high and sell it cheap' policy may mean more people in the short term, but the long-term risks are great. The image of the islands has already been badly damaged, while similar islands which cultivate an up-market image (such as Madeira) – even though they may have less to offer than the Canaries –

Time-share and concrete canyons (Puerto Rico, Gran Canaria) have had a dramatic effect on the life of the Canary Islands

consistently attract higher-spending tourists, who in the long run are more profitable.

Profitable operations need not resort to bland international mediocrity, as much of Lanzarote, the island *paradores* and such establishments as the Hotel Tecina on La Gomera prove. In the wake of the recent world recession it seems unlikely that the Canary Islands will grasp this nettle in the short term. Whether the hoteliers and authorities will eventually kill the Canaries that lay the golden eggs remains to be seen.

Politics

*I*n 1982 the Canary Islands were granted autonomy (the right to self-government) as part of the general Spanish policy of decentralisation. Their government is conducted jointly from the two capitals of Las Palmas (for the eastern islands) and Santa Cruz de Tenerife (for the western islands). Las Palmas has been assigned half of the regional government departments and the islands' Supreme Court, while Santa Cruz has the other half of the departments and the Parliament. Each of the two provinces has a governor appointed by Madrid.

Representation and structure
The Canarian Parliament comprises 15 members from Gran Canaria, 15 members from Tenerife, eight from La Palma, eight from Lanzarote, seven from Fuerteventura, four from La Gomera and three from El Hierro. In addition to its legislative role, it sets island budgets and appoints representatives to take its case to the mainland.

Each island also has its own island council, known as the *Cabildo Insular*, which possesses certain powers of self-government and accepts responsibility for the daily running of local services. These functions are in turn delegated to *municipios* (regional municipal units), then finally to town authorities, whose *ayuntamiento* (town hall) is usually a handsome traditional building in the central square.

The independence movement
The most obvious sign of Canarian discontent with the mainland is roadside graffiti spelling 'Spanish Go Home' or 'Godos Out'. 'Godos' (literally meaning 'Goths') refers to Spanish island workers, convenient scapegoats accused of taking jobs from the locals. This does, of course, happen in some cases, but the 'Godos' also provide skills lost in previous bouts of emigration, when the most willing and most able islanders went to South America in search of a better future.

The main independence party is the AIC (Association of Canary Independents), which carries around one-third of the popular vote. Its aims are moderate, directed more towards greater autonomy than towards full independence.

The three flags of authority in the islands: Spain (left), the Canaries (centre) and the European Union (right). Although self-governing, the Canary Islands remain Spanish and as such they have extended membership of the EU

FIRST STEPS

*The blue sky and
all-pervading sun overhead,
the delicious warmth
but exquisite freshness of
the air, all tell us
that we have reached the
haven of our rest...the
Fortunate Islands.*

ERNEST HART
*Letter to the British Medical
Journal about Tenerife in 1887*

Life on the smaller islands moves at a slow pace – goatherd on La Gomera

Over the last three decades the Canary Islands have become as well known as the Spanish *costas* for a budget family playground of sun, sea and sand. It is true that this type of holiday can be found in abundance in the southern resorts of Tenerife, Gran Canaria and in certain parts of Lanzarote and Fuerteventura. But elsewhere on the islands there are few family tourism facilities, surprisingly little sand, and away from the southern shores even the sun is not always reliable. All this means fewer people, which to some holidaymakers is an attraction in itself.

Which island?

If you're the social type and like to be among people of your own nationality, drinking in the types of bars you find at home and with all facilities laid on, then the above mentioned resorts are for you. The highlights of all islands are well catered for by coach trips, so you don't even have to hire a car.

There's little to choose between Gran Canaria and Tenerife in terms of overall appeal. The former takes the lead in terms of beaches; the latter has more man-made attractions to enjoy. If you're still confused and think that the southern resorts of the big two islands sound over-commercialised, then Lanzarote may be the best choice. Fuerteventura is an island for beach-lovers and watersport fans. There's little else to see or do there. At the other extreme, if you're the solitary type who takes pleasure in lonely walks, landscapes and quiet local bars, one of the minor islands may well be your scene (though El Hierro may be a little too quiet for most).

Of course, it's possible to get the best of both worlds – there is a handful of luxury hotels on La Gomera and La Palma which make 'going native' very painless. Or you could try self-catering on one of the larger islands, somewhere away from the larger resorts. Good accommodation for the independent traveller, however, is not easy to find.

Island-hopping

There is no tradition of island-hopping in the Canaries, as there is on the Greek Islands. This is due to the distances involved, the packaged nature of Canarian holidays, which means few good budget hotels, and the packaged image of the islands, which in itself attracts a less adventurous type of traveller. Two-centre holidays are about as far as the genre goes. Tenerife/La Gomera and Lanzarote/Fuerteventura are the favourite combinations, due to their proximity and 35-minute sailing times, but it is possible to reach any of

Rural and urban images: fieldworker on Tenerife (above); street sign on Gran Canaria (left)

the islands in under 45 minutes' flying time. Inter-island flights go via Gran Canaria for the eastern islands and Tenerife (Los Rodeos, north airport), for the western islands. All islands have their own airport (La Gomera's is currently under construction near Playa de Santiago in the south). Fares are very reasonable, check-in times are short and it's an ideal way to sample the smaller islands for a day or two before committing yourself to a longer stay.

The black volcanic sands of Playa de las Américas, Tenerife

doesn't mean that you should assume everyone speaks English. A little Spanish will always be appreciated and it's essential if you want to order something that is not on view or ask what's cooking in the kitchen; in village bars they don't always have menus, or even food on display, but they'll usually be pleased to cook you a snack.

Don't forget the old tradition of the *siesta*. Villages and towns close down for the afternoon from around 1pm to 4 or 5pm. This isn't a good time to explore any settlement as churches, local museums and shops will all be closed and there will be a general ghost town atmosphere. It's much better to arrive in the early evening, when the Spanish tradition of the *paseo* (the promenade, or evening stroll) brings families out in their finery, and a lively atmosphere prevails in bars and cafés. When the *paseo* finishes, it is time to eat. The evening meal is generally taken around 8pm, a little later than in northern Europe, though early by much of Spanish mainland standards.

Cultural differences

If you're familiar with mainland Spain then you won't find too much to surprise you in the Canary Islands. Tourism is so well established on all the islands except El Hierro that you'll very rarely have a problem making yourself understood or finding what you want. However, this

WHAT'S IN A NAME

Surprising as it may seem, the Canary Islands are not named after the tiny yellow finch-like bird that inhabit the islands. In fact, it is the reverse, the birds take their name from the islands (they also live on the other Macaronesian islands; see pages 12–13). If you want to glimpse a rare canary in the wild, look among stands of canary pines, but you'll have a much better chance of seeing them kept in cages outside village houses on Gran Canaria and Tenerife.

The most enduring legend associated with the name of the islands is that they were named after native dogs (*canes*, Spanish for canines) found by early Mauretanian explorers. Today's *verdino*, the native Canarian dog, is presumably a descendant. If you don't see any real *verdinos*, look out for the famous statues by the cathedral in Las Palmas on Gran Canaria..

WHAT TO SEE

The island fell away below
us in a mighty sweep. . .
hundreds of houses
spangled the deep green
landscape, like white
pearls scattered with a
lavish hand. . .
What coastal scenery!

HERMAN CHRIST,
SWISS BOTANIST
Spring Journey to the Canaries, 1886

Gran Canaria

*D*espite its name and fame, Gran Canaria isn't the biggest of the Canaries, yet somehow it feels big. In Las Palmas it has the most populous and dynamic city on the archipelago; Maspalomas is one of the largest resort complexes in Europe, and the inland scenery is grand in every sense. Only Tenerife can match its combination of cosmopolitan, rural and seaside attractions, and there is no question that the beaches of Gran Canaria are superior.

The island's comparatively small size can also be an advantage. Both Las Palmas and Maspalomas are just 30 minutes from the airport and nowhere on the island is over an hour's drive from either of these destinations. In fact it's quite possible to drive round the whole island in a day.

Gran Canaria is the most popular island after Tenerife, but if you do wish to get away from it all you needn't worry about tourist hordes. The majority of visitors simply flop on to their towels and stay there.

Gran Canaria is often called 'a continent in miniature'; a reference to the extremes of landscape and climate that may be found on this island. Its landscapes change quickly from Wild West canyons to idyllic pine forests to Sahara-like dunes, and while there may be a dusting of snow on Pico de las Nieves, Maspalomas will still be wallowing in sun. Gran Canaria is also culturally and historically the most well endowed of the islands. The best performing arts and museums are in Las Palmas, and a rich collection of Guanche sites and relics is scattered around the island.

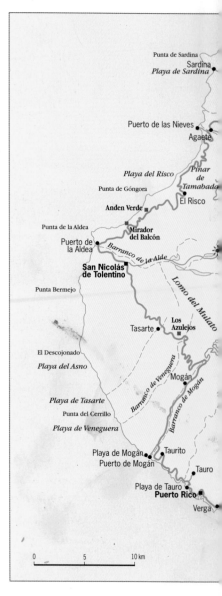

GRAN CANARIA

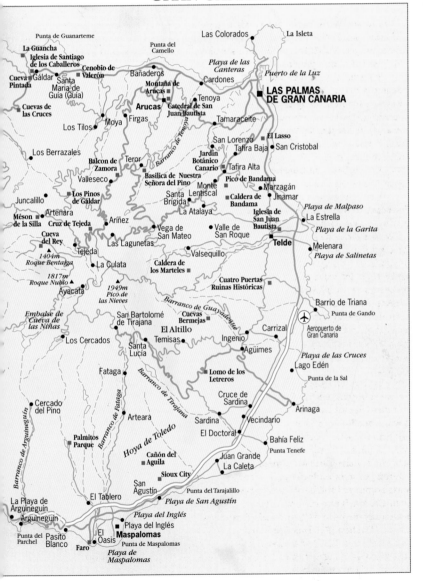

Central Gran Canaria

*T*he heart of the island was once a sacred point for the Guanches, and their totem rocks, Nublo and Bentayga, still dominate an epic mountain landscape. Breathtaking *miradores* (lookout points) are the hallmark of this area, peering down to all points of the island and beyond.

ARTENARA

At an altitude of 1,200m, this peaceful whitewashed settlement is certainly the highest and arguably the most spectacular village on the island, clinging to the mountainside. The views across the ravine, either from the pretty terrace of the Méson de Silla restaurant or from the square next to the church, are legendary. Not so well known, however, is the village's small cave-church (up the hill, opposite the main church).
18km northwest of Cruz de Tejeda.

CRUZ DE TEJEDA

The Cruz de Tejeda is a busy crossroads where you will find all sorts of merchandise and refreshment, including the island's *parador* (see pages 170-3, no accommodation available). Here, at an altitude of 1,490m, there are marvellous views of three major landmarks: Roque Bentaiga, Roque Nublo and Mount Teide, on Tenerife. Don't miss the *cruz* (cross) itself – a finely carved stone cross in front of the *parador* terrace. Close by, the village of Tejeda enjoys a picturesque position among verdant hills.
43km southwest of Las Palmas, 45km north of Maspalomas.

LOS PINOS DE GÁLDAR

The *mirador* of 'the pines of Gáldar' is a

Enhanced by the early light of dawn Roque Bentaiga displays a primordial landscape

vantage point unlike many in the mountainous interior. Here the view stumbles over the edge of a crater, slides down verdant pine-covered hillsides and descends for over 40km, taking in the whole of the north coast.
9km north of Cruz de Tejeda.

PICO DE LAS NIEVES
The 'Peak of the Snows' is the geographic centre and highest point of Gran Canaria, at 1,949m above sea-level. Cloud permitting, the views of the island's mountainous interior are superb from here.
8km southeast of Cruz de Tejeda.

PINAR DE TAMADABA
The *pinar* (pine forest) of Tamadaba is a beautiful area of tall, slender pines to the northwest of Artenara. A narrow circular road snakes up to around 1,400m and, if the weather is clear, rewards you with a priceless view of Mount Teide, floating above the clouds.
25km northwest of Cruz de Tejeda.

ROQUE BENTAIGA/CUEVA DEL REY
Roque Bentaiga was a sacred spot to the Guanches, and goats were once sacrificed on the simple altar which still stands here. It's possible to walk up to the summit (1,404m) but you must be very sure-footed and have a head for heights. Along the same track (past the Bentaiga turning) is the Cueva del Rey (King's Cave). Stop your car when a tall crag looms to your left and the road dives downhill to your right. Walk round the mountainside to your left and the Cueva del Rey, once the royal abode, is high above in the honeycombed rock. The views from here, across to Artenara, are truly fit for a king. It is possible to climb

The Cross of Tejeda – yesterday's pilgrimage point is today's tourist attraction

right up to the caves but be very careful if you do.

As if to confirm the Guanches' mystic views, from certain angles, the rock next to Bentaiga takes on the appearance of a robed holy man – hence its name, Roque El Fraile ('The Monk').
Location: on the C-811 between Cruz de Tejeda and Ayacata (44km from Las Palmas).

ROQUE NUBLO (Cloud Rock)
It is claimed that this landmark pinnacle, pointing 1,803m into the Canarian sky, is the world's highest basalt monolith. Like Roque Bentaiga, this, too, was once a holy site. If you want to walk to the rock it's just over 6km from the nearest accessible approach point of La Culata.
La Culata is 1km north of Ayacata.

Eastern Gran Canaria

*I*t may be hard to believe that there is life beyond the soulless strip of the GC1 motorway and barren east coast, but just a few kilometres inland are wealthy villages, a sub-tropical *barranco* (ravine), a colonised crater and the island's second city.

BANDAMA (CALDERA DE/PICO DE)

The volcano of Bandama rises to 569m and is a popular *mirador*, with views straight down into the crater (see pages 48–9) and across to Las Palmas. The adjacent Golf Club de Bandama enjoys a magnificent setting.
10km south of Las Palmas.

BARRANCO DE GUAYADEQUE

The lush and spectacular ravine of Guayadeque drains almost from the centre of the island to the coast. From the visitor's viewpoint, however, it starts gradually at Agüimes, with banana plantations, which give way to tall palms and wild cacti as the valley sides grow in height. After 5km the Cuevas Bermejas (Purple Caves) are the first sign that this

was once a Guanche stronghold. Here, latter-day troglodytes have their homes, keep their animals and have built a cave chapel.

Soon, the valley sides rise to 300m high and in spring the area is a riot of pink almond blossom. After another 3km the road ends at the Montaña de las Tierras, where there are more caves (old and new) and refreshments.
Just outside Agüimes (14km south of Telde). On the road in from the GC1 look for a small sign on the right-hand side before Agüimes centre.

INGENIO

Ingenio is a prosperous market town and also boasts a tradition of handicrafts. You can visit some of the town's *artesanías* (craft workshops) on the main road towards Telde (the C816 road). Also on this road, just outside town, is the Museo de Piedras y Artesanía Canaria (Museum of Rocks and Canarian handicrafts). It's a strange mix of old-fashioned geological exhibits, bygones, embroidery and gaudy religious displays.
Ingenio is 12km south of Telde. Museum: open daily 9am–6pm. Admission free.

JARDÍN (BOTÁNICO) CANARIO

This is the island's most comprehensive garden, laid out in 1952 on a steep hillside, with as near natural conditions

Barranco de Guaydeque, seen from Montaña de las Tierras

Telde's wealth of Spanish colonial buildings is the legacy of 16th-century sugar-cane traders

as possible. Here you can see virtually every type of plant indigenous to the island grouping of Macaronesia (see pages 10–11).

La Calzada, near Tafira Alta, 7km southwest of Las Palmas. Open: Monday to Friday 8am–noon and 3–6pm, Saturday 8am–noon and 1–5.30pm, Sunday 10am–noon and 3–5pm. Admission free.

TAFIRA/SANTA BRÍGIDA/VEGA DE SAN MATEO

This triumvirate of villages, already prosperous from the rich farming communities around them, has been colonised by the well-to-do of Las Palmas. Vega de San Mateo is the most interesting of the three, with a busy Sunday livestock market and the ethnological museum of Casa de Cho Zacharías, with a collection of agricultural equipment and craft work. Aside from this there is little formal sightseeing, but the area provides a pleasant drive out from Las Palmas, past handsome villas, expensive restaurants and views down into verdant valleys.

Southwest of Las Palmas, Tafira 8km, Santa Brígida 15km, Vega de San Mateo 20km. Museum (tel: 64 06 27). Open: daily, 9.30am–1pm (telephone to arrange visits with guide).

TELDE

Gran Canaria's second city owes its wealth to its 16th-century sugar-cane trade, and grand mansions of this period can be found in the San Juan district to the north of the town. In the same quarter is the jewel of the city – the richly decorated 15th-century Iglesia de San Juan de Bautista (Church of St John the Baptist). It has a splendidly carved early 16th-century Flemish altarpiece and, from the same period, an intriguing life-size figure of Christ, made in Mexico from corn husks and weighing just 5 kg.

The rest of Telde is a poorly signposted, traffic-clogged city which holds little for visitors.

14km south of Las Palmas. The Church of St John the Baptist is in the Plaza de San Juan Bautista and is open for services only.

Las Palmas

*L*as Palmas, the biggest city on the archipelago (population 366,000) is a major port, an historic capital, a business centre and a holiday resort. Not so long ago it was *the* fashionable Canarian resort but nowadays most holiday-makers head to the purpose-built southern developments, where sunshine is virtually guaranteed and a 'real British Pub' is never far away.

Las Palmas is not to everyone's taste. It's busy, noisy, run-down in parts and suffers from petty crime and traffic problems. But there is more Spanish atmosphere, history and culture to enjoy here than anywhere else on the island.
Las Palmas is 58km north of Maspalomas. Tourist office: Parque de Santa Catalina (tel: 26 46 23). Open: Monday to Friday, 9am–1.30pm and 5pm–7pm; Saturday, 9.30am–1pm.

CASA DE COLÓN (House of Columbus)

The House of Columbus belonged to the island's first governor, and dates originally from the 15th century. Columbus stayed here on either two or three occasions en route to the New World. The house is now an atmospheric museum with paintings and artefacts relating to his journeys. The other side of the building houses a Museum of Fine Art.
Calle de Colón 1, Vegueta (tel: 31 12 55). Open: Monday to Friday, 9am–2pm; Saturday, 9am–1pm. Closed Sunday and public holidays. Admission charge.

CATEDRAL DE SANTA ANA (Cathedral of St Ana)

From the outside there is little to commend this huge, grimy building. Construction began in 1497 but it was still being built in the 20th century. Inside, however, there are many treasures. The highlight is its Museo Diocesano de

Arte Sacro (Diocesan Museum of Sacred Art), boasting a rich collection of statues, paintings and gold and silver ware.

The Plaza de Santa Ana in front of the cathedral is a handsome square with the *ayuntamiento* (Town Hall) at the far end and to the right, the Palacio Episcopal (Bishop's Palace).
Plaza de Santa Ana (tel: 31 36 00). Museum open: Monday to Friday, 9am–1.30pm and 4–8pm; Saturday, 9am–2pm. Admission charge.

DORAMAS PARQUE/PUEBLO CANARIO (Canary Village)

The centrepiece of this pleasant, grassy park is the Pueblo Canario, an idealised re-creation of a typical village, including a church, a *bodega* (wine bar), shops, a tourist office and the Museo de Néstor (see below), arranged around a pretty square. Come here on Sunday between 11.30am and 1pm, or Thursday between 5.30pm and 7.00pm, when a folk group entertains with song and dance.

Néstor de la Torre was a famous local artist and designer, who conceived, among other projects, the Pueblo Canario. The Museo de Néstor features many of his best exotic Symbolist paintings.
Pueblo Canario (tel: 24 51 35). Open: Tuesday to Friday, 10am–1pm and 4–8pm; Sunday, 11am–2pm. Admission charge. Tourist Office (tel: 24 35 93). Open: Monday to Friday, 9am–1.30pm and 5pm–7pm; Saturday, 9.30am–1pm.

LAS PALMAS DE GRAN CANARIA

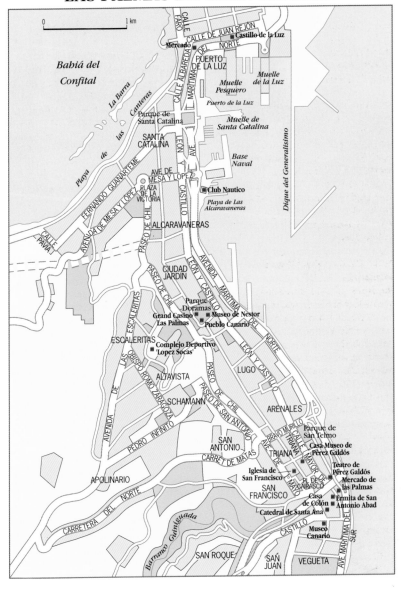

0   1 km

Bahiá del
Confital

La Barra

Playa de las Canteras

Playa de

CALLE FARO

CALLE DE JUAN REJÓN

Mercado

Castillo de la Luz

AVENIDA DEL NORTE

PUERTO
DE LA LUZ

CALLE ALBAREDA

Muelle
Pesquero

Muelle
de la Luz

Puerto de la Luz

Parque de
Santa Catalina

Muelle de
Santa Catalina

SANTA
CATALINA

CALLE MARÍTIMA

LEÓN Y

AVE.

Base
Naval

Dique del Generalísimo

FERNANDO GUANARTEME

AVE DE
MESA Y LOPEZ

CASTILLO

Club Nautico

PLAZA
DE LA
VICTORIA

Playa de Las
Alcaravaneras

AVENIDA DE MESA Y LOPEZ

PASEO DE CHIL

ALCARAVANERAS

CALLE
PAVIA

AVENIDA MARÍTIMA DEL NORTE

PASEO DE CHIL

CIUDAD
JARDIN

LEÓN Y CASTILLO

ESCALERITAS

Parque
Doramas

Grand Casino
Las Palmas

Museo de Nestor

Pueblo Canario

ESCALERITAS

DE

OBISPO ROMO ZARAGOZA

Complejo Deportivo
'Lopez Socás'

LUGO

ALTAVISTA

AVENIDA

PASEO DE SAN ANTONIO

PASEO DE CHIL

SCHAMANN

LEÓN Y CASTILLO

ARENALES

PEDRO INFINITO

BRAVO MURILLO

AVE. PRIMERO DE MAYO

Parque de
San Telmo

SAN
ANTONIO

CALLE TRIANA

Casa Museo de
Pérez Galdós

CARRET DE MATAS

CALLE MAYOR

Teatro de
Pérez Galdós

APOLINARIO

Iglesia de
San Francisco

SAN
FRANCISCO

PL. DE
CAIRASCO

Casa
de Colón

Mercado de
las Palmas

Ermita de San
Antonio Abad

CARRETERA DEL NORTE

Catedral de Santa Ana

CASTILLO

Museo
Canario

AVE. MARÍTIMA DEL SUR

Barranco Guiniguada

SAN ROQUE

SAN
JUAN

VEGUETA

The sombre façade of the Catedral de Santa Ana in the Vegueta Quarter of Las Palmas

MUSEO CANARIO (Canary Islands Museum)

This rather old-fashioned museum holds the finest collection of Guanche artefacts in the whole archipelago. Along with everyday grave finds, there is a startling display of skulls and mummies, which will delight older children.

Calle Dr Verneau 2 (tel: 31 56 00). Open: Monday to Friday, 10am–1pm and 4pm–7.30pm; Saturday, 10am–1pm; Sunday, 10am–2pm. Admission charge.

PLAYA DE LAS CANTERAS

This long, golden crescent-shaped beach is one of the longest city beaches in the worlds extending for 2.6km on the NW side of Las Palmas. It is conveniently protected from Atlantic rollers by a natural reef close to the shore, and is ideal for safe bathing. Those in need of wind and waves need only venture out beyond the reef. The promenade is lined with restaurants of many nationalities – Bulgarian, Korean and Japanese sit alongside British, German and Swedish eating houses, reflecting the home countries of the sailors who take 'rest and recreation' here alongside ordinary holidaymakers.

PUERTO DE LA LUZ

Las Palmas was once one of the busiest ports in the western hemisphere. Today it still throbs, with up to 1,000 ships a month passing through, but it has lost much of its vitality. The number of sailors has diminished as the nature of cargo-handling has become less labour-intensive and few ocean-liners now call here.

The port is at its most colourful on Sunday mornings, when the *rastro* (flea-market) on the Avenida Marítima is patronised by locals, tourists and a good number of West African shoppers and vendors. Near by, in Calle de Juan Rejón, the sturdy stone Castillo de la Luz (castle), built in 1494, is the oldest building on Gran Canaria. It is occasionally open for special exhibitions (enquire at the tourist office).

SANTA CATALINA
This is the bustling area behind the beach, jam-packed with duty-free shops, hotels, restaurants, bars and the red-light district. The hub of the area is the cosmopolitan garden square of Parque de Santa Catalina. Here you will find Europeans, Africans and North Americans enjoying a drink and indulging in the park's favourite pastime of people-watching.

TRIANA
Triana is the city's original commercial district. The area's main thoroughfare is the pedestrianised shopping street of Calle Mayor de Triana. At its northern end is the charming Parque de San Telmo, with a chapel and some fine dragon trees. Towards the southern end of the street at no 6 Calle Cano lies the Casa Museo de Pérez Galdós, former home of one of the island's favourite writers, born here in 1843. The handsome 1919 Teatro de Pérez Galdós opera house is close by.

Just off the north end of Calle Mayor are the beautiful squares of San Francisco and Cairasco. The former houses a fine bust of Columbus and the lovely 17th-century Iglesia de San Francisco. The Plaza de Cairasco is notable for the 100-year-old Gabinete Literario (Literary Cabinet Institute), elegantly arcaded and stuccoed and occasionally open to the public for exhibitions (enquire at tourist office).

Casa Museo de Pérez Galdós, Calle Cano, 6 (tel: 36 69 76). Open: Monday to Saturday, 9am–2pm. Admission free.

VEGUETA QUARTER
This is the oldest part of town, where the Castilian conquerors landed in 1478, and became the district where the ruling classes lived. It still retains an aristocratic air, with splendid 17th- and 18th-century mansions decorated with coats of arms and elegantly crafted balconies. The shady squares and worn cobbled streets have changed little since Columbus's day and you can visit the Casa de Colón, where he stayed (see above) and see the Ermita (Church) de San Antonio Abad, where he prayed. The latter was rebuilt in the 18th century but is rarely open to the public. Vegueta is also home to the Catedral de Santa Ana (see page 32).

The golden crescent of Canteras Beach

CHRISTOPHER COLUMBUS

Christopher Columbus (Cristóbal Colón in Spanish) used the Canary Islands as a staging post on several occasions for his voyages to the New World. The records of his visits vary and different sources argue about where he was on any one occasion. There is agreement, however, that he did stop off at Las Palmas and La Gomera in 1492.

On Gran Canaria Colombus may have dropped anchor at Gando Bay (where the airport now is) or near the site of the present-day Puerto de la Luz in Las Palmas. From his own diary we know that just as he was passing

Tenerife, Mount Teide erupted, and this was taken as an ill omen by his superstitious crew.

Columbus also stopped at La Gomera to take on water and other supplies, but another reason he may have wanted to stop here was to see the Countess of Gomera, Beatriz de Bobadilla (see page 111). Columbus probaby knew her from the Spanish Court – he was sailing under the flag of Ferdinand and Isabella – and there are

(Above): an 18th-century engraving of the first voyage; (far left) statue in the Fundacion César Manrique; (left) Columbus's house, Las Palmas

rumours of an affair.

Columbus may have returned to La Gomera on his voyages of 1493–5 and 1498–1500. It is also thought that he visited Las Palmas on at least two occasions (either during the aforementioned dates or on his last voyage of 1502–4).

Other records mention Maspalomas on Gran Canaria and El Hierro as stopping points.

Local latter-day reactions to the great explorer are mixed. While Gran Canarios don't seem unduly disturbed by modern interpretations of Columbus as hero or villain (Colón is, after all, derived from the Spanish word for 'colonialism'), Gomerans take a sterner view. They no doubt remember that Columbus was involved with the slave trade, and was, at the very least, friendly with the Countess Beatriz, who tyrannised the island. Graffiti protesting against the celebrations which marked the 500th anniversary of the 'Discovery' could be seen in the island capital in 1992. The resistance to the Spanish Conquest was as fierce on La Gomera as anywhere. It seems that memories here are also very long.

Maspalomas

*A*s surely as nature has created the rugged interior of Gran Canaria, so developers have created the streamlined holiday world of Maspalomas – the 'Costa Canaria'. It will either distress or reassure you to learn that this is one of the three biggest resort complexes under the Spanish flag, on the same scale as Benidorm and Torremolinos. First impressions are inauspicious, as serried ranks of high-rise towers loom next to the motorway. Beyond this however most of the developments are nearer the ground and the beaches are the finest on the island.

DUNAS DE MASPALOMAS (Dunes of Maspalomas)

Spectacular golden-white dunes are the trademark of this area. Despite their Saharan appearance they were not blown in from Africa (as was once thought), nor were they shipped here as a tourist attraction (as was Las Teresitas beach on Tenerife). They are a product of sea and wind forces peculiar to this area. The dunes have always been protected from development, but anybody is free to walk across them. Don't be surprised if you are confronted by nudists or a tourist camel train; both use the dunes frequently. One of the best views of the dunes is at sunset from the terrace of the Hotel Riu Palace in Playa del Inglés.

The desert-like sand dunes of Maspalomas

MASPALOMAS (Faro)

Rather confusingly, the name Maspalomas refers not only to the larger Costa Canaria conurbation, but to the original oasis area of Maspalomas, which also includes Playa del Inglés and San Agustín. Until the early 1960s this was simply an oasis by the dunes with a freshwater pool, a palm grove and a lighthouse (faro), which dates from 1886. All of this remains, but nowadays the oasis is the preserve of luxury hotels. Hotel guests here enjoy a beach with an exotic backdrop, more intimate than the long featureless stretches just to the east. The rest of Maspalomas – largely self-catering bungalows – clusters around a championship golf course, before merging almost imperceptibly into Playa del Inglés.

The resort's biggest man-made attraction is Holiday World, a large amusement park (and the first in the Canaries) in a pleasant garden setting. Here there are all the usual favourites: a landmark ferris wheel, swingboats, bumping cars (and boats), phantom jets and so on. Newer innovations include a parrot show and a laser-battle game.
Maspalomas Faro is 58km south of Las Palmas. For Tourist Information see Playa del Inglés. Holiday World is open Tuesday to Sunday, 5pm–1am. Admission charge (covers all rides).

PASITO BLANCO

This new marina development with berthing room for up to 500 pleasure craft occupies a pretty cove. Big-game fishing boats can be hired and it's always interesting to see the catches being proudly exhibited late in the afternoon.
6km west of Maspalomas Faro.

PLAYA DEL INGLÉS

The name of this resort, 'Beach of the

The Ecumenical Church at Playa del Inglés

English', is somewhat misleading; you will find many different north European nationalities here. It was created from scratch on barren land during the 1960s and has become a super-compressed labyrinth of hotels, apartments, cheap restaurants, bars and ugly *Centro Commerciales* (shopping centres). The only points of sightseeing interest are the intriguing Ecumenical Church, which resembles a portion of the Sydney Opera House, and the Insular Tourism Center, which doubles as a tourist information and cultural centre. Here handicrafts are on sale and local musicians give concerts. The resort beach is long, golden, windswept and has every facility, including a Macdonald's burger bar.
5km east of Maspalomas Faro. Insular Tourism Center: Avenida España/Estados Unidos (tel: 76 78 48). Open: Monday to Saturday; shops, 9am–1pm and 4pm–7pm; tourist office, 9am–9pm.

The lush, fertile oasis town of Fataga is situated in a barren mountainous landscape

SAN AGUSTÍN

Although the very first hotel on the Costa Canaria sprang up here in the early 1960s, San Agustín has remained the most restrained of the three resorts. It is largely given over to low-rise apartments with attractive gardens and draws an older clientèle, who don't seem to mind that their beach is the darkest coloured of the three, though it does have the advantage of a low cliff backing.
9km east of Maspalomas Faro.

SIOUX CITY

This 'paella-Western' theme park occupies a canyon with genuine Wild West scenery. Stunt men act out bank hold-ups, shoot-outs and lynchings, Mexican *hombres* perform knife-throwing acts and a routine from the saloon gals and boys reduces the adrenaline before a cowboy barbecue.
3km north of San Agustín. No 29 bus. Cañon del Aguila (tel: 76 25 73). Open: Monday to Saturday. Shows (Knife-throwing, shooting and lassoing etc) at noon and 6pm. Western night barbecue dinner Friday, 8pm. Admission charge.

Near Maspalomas

FATAGA

This charming oasis settlement lies in the middle of the 'Valley of a Thousand Palms'. A handful of whitewashed houses and shops, a small archetypal church, a bar and a restaurant comprise the prettiest small village on the island. The adjacent palm-filled Barranco de Fataga is popular for its camel farms and camel safaris.
20km north of Maspalomas Faro.

PALMITOS PARQUE

Set in beautifully landscaped gardens in a dramatic canyon, this is the finest bird park on the islands. The caged birds are well displayed, with abundant greenery softening the feeling of captivity, but what makes this park special is the number of free-flying species. It's exhilarating to see toucans and other brightly coloured birds flying and nesting in the palms above.

There's also a parrot-show and one of the biggest butterfly houses in Europe, with hundreds of tropical varieties flying freely.

10km north of Maspalomas Faro (tel: 14 22 28). No 45 bus. Open: daily, 9am–6pm. Admission charge.

SAN BARTOLOMÉ DE TIRAJANA

The rustic streets and earthy bars of this small agricultural village are a perfect antidote to the contrived resort life of the coast. The best time to visit is on a Sunday morning, when a lively market takes place. The present village church dates from 1903, and contains a statue of St James (Santiago) which was held in the 15th-century hermitage on the same site. It shows Santiago in his traditional Spanish role as 'Moor-slayer' and was brought here during the Conquest in the hope that it would have the same evangelising effect on the Guanches. Walk up the hill and you will find many old houses. The House of Tunte (the Guanche name for the village) and the Corner of Tunte in Princesa Guayarmina alleyway date from the 15th century.

28km north of Maspalomas Faro.

SANTA LUCÍA DE TIRAJANA

From San Bartolomé the road snakes down to the east, through a fertile valley to the pretty village of Santa Lucía. The church here is a landmark for miles

Palmitos Parque is a showcase for native flora and fauna

around, with a large, white Moorish dome. In front are luxurious, well-tended gardens. A little way past the village is the private Museo Castillo de la Fortaleza. The castle in question is a new, small mock-fortress with dusty displays on archaeology, fossils and ethnography (including a 16th-century bedroom), among other exhibits. Don't miss the fine display of paintings upstairs. The museum boasts a lovely garden, complete with rusting cannons and a charming outdoor restaurant.

Santa Lucía is 31km north of Maspalomas Faro. The church is open: Monday to Saturday, 10am–5pm; Sunday, noon–4pm. Admission charge. The museum is on the C815 road, 1km north of the village (tel: 79 83 10). Open: daily, 9am–6.30pm. Admission charge.

Northern Gran Canaria

*I*f you are in search of typical Gran Canarian settlements, head north. The small towns and villages here are self-contained farming communities and rely neither on tourism nor on the wealth of Las Palmas. The coast road provides spectacular views down to the wild northwest fringes and across to Tenerife.

AGAETE

This picturesque, small town lies in a particularly fertile belt, with coffee and exotic fruits among its many crops. The showpiece, Huerto de las Flores (Garden of the Flowers), a garden of tropical and sub-tropical plants, demonstrates what is possible. In the town square old men doze on park benches in front of the large, red-domed church.

The port of Agaete, Puerto de las Nieves, is a windswept spot with a small promenade overlooking wild cliff scenery and a black pebble beach with fishing boats. A famous rock stack here goes by the name of Dedo de Dios (Finger of God).

41km west of Las Palmas. Huerto de las Flores is a small enclosed park in the centre of the village. Open: dawn until dusk. Admission free.

ARUCAS

A towering, neo-gothic cathedral is the last thing you would expect to see in the midst of a whitewashed Canarian farming community. It was started in 1909 and completed in the late 1970s as an ostentatious sign of the town's wealth – founded in no small part on the locally produced rum, *(ron)* on sale on all the islands. Near the church is a small botanic garden (the Parque Municipal) and a statue to the Guanche king, Doramas. Legend has it that he was slain treacherously while challenging the conquistador Pedro de Vera to single combat on Montaña de Arucas in 1481. This provides the dramatic backdrop to the town and a road from the church leads to the mountain.

17km west of Las Palmas.

GÁLDAR

This busy, workaday town, once the

'God's Finger' at Puerto de las Nieves

capital of the island, has several points of interest. In the main square, look inside the courtyard of the Town Hall (open weekday mornings only), where the ancient dragon tree is said to be the oldest on the island. Ask here about visiting arrangements for the Cueva Pintada (see below). Also in the square is the Iglesia de Santiago de los Caballeros, a church dating from 1872 and containing many fine sculptures.

The Cueva Pintada (Painted Cave), at the southwest end of town, is a small Guanche cave with painted geometric figures, only discovered in 1873 and unique to the islands. It has, however, been closed to the public for many years while undergoing restoration work. The other Guanche legacy near by (on the road leading to La Guancha) is an 11th-century cemetery. It is thought to be the last resting place of Guanche nobles. Today it is in a neglected state, enclosed behind a wire fence.
31km west of Las Palmas

(SANTA MARIA DE) GUÍA

In the centre of Guía is a pretty square with an imposing neo-classical church and narrow streets running off it. The main attraction, however, is the Cenobio de Valerón (Convent of Valeron) just to the east of town. This is a honeycomb of Guanche caves set in a sheer rock face, to which new concrete steps (190 in all!) offer access (though visitors are not allowed inside the caves). Despite fanciful legends that these were once priestesses' and virgins' lodgings, the caves were probably just a grain store.
28km west of Las Palmas. Caves open: Tuesday to Sunday, 10am–1pm and 3pm–5pm. Admission free.

TEROR

Architecturally this is the most typical

God's house at Arucas

Canarian town on the island, with beautifully preserved white houses and dozens of perfectly carved wooden balconies. It is also the religious centre of Gran Canaria, with a statue of the Virgin housed in the town's splendid 18th-century basilica. The only house open to the public is the atmospheric 17th-century Casa de los Patronos de la Virgen del Pino, which is now a museum of bygones with a beautiful patio.

The best time to visit Teror is on a Sunday morning, when the local market is in full cry.
23km southwest of Las Palmas. Museum (tel: 63 02 39). Open: Monday to Thursday, 11am–6.30pm; Saturday, 11am–5.45pm; Sunday, 10am–2pm. Admission charge.

Western Gran Canaria

*U*ntil quite recently the west of Gran Canaria was little visited, and even today the coast north of Puerto de Mogán is undeveloped. The southwest corner, however, is a conservationist's nightmare, with row upon row of white boxes obscuring the hillsides. The development of Puerto de Mogán itself partly redresses these excesses, while the natural scenery beyond it is spectacular.

ARGUINEGUÍN

Arguineguín, not to be confused with the adjacent La Playa de Arguineguín/ Patalavaca tourist development, is the only genuine fishing village on this part of the coast. Market day, Tuesday, is the best time to visit but there is a daily fish auction at the port.

12km west of Maspalomas.

MOGÁN

This small, pretty, quiet hill village is a breath of fresh air after the overcrowded coastal strip – its gardens and countryside abound with tropical fruits and flowers.

For a memorable picnic, take the minor C811 road 10km north to the beautifully situated Embalse de Cueva de las Niñas ('The Little Girls' Cave Reservoir'), where there are benches and barbecue facilities.

Another point of outstanding natural beauty, Los Azulejos, lies 11km north of Mogán on the road to San Nicolás. This is a spectacular cliff, worn away to reveal a veined and striped cross-section of reds, yellows, blues and greens.

Mogán is 9km north of Puerto de Mogán.

PUERTO DE MOGÁN

Puerto de Mogán is a model example of sympathetic Canarian holiday development. The old fishing harbour has been expanded to a traffic-free 'village' of local-style houses, painted white with a pastel trim, each with a wrought-iron balcony and pretty window boxes or garden. The houses cluster around a new pleasure marina, joined coherently by arches and bridges, and shops, bars and restaurants are well-kept.

The original fishing fleet is still here and gives a genuine local touch to the marina. There is a small black beach next to the port but most visitors prefer

PUTTING TO SEA

Most holidaymakers on this coast will be tempted on to at least one sea excursion. Options include a lazy day on the fully rigged *Windjammer San Miguel*, a shark-fishing adventure or a *Yellow Submarine* voyage. The latter is certainly the most novel ride, but it is expensive and aside from a couple of wrecks, there is little to see. The *Lineas Salmon* boat provides a useful regular transport service between Arguineguín, Puerto Rico and Puerto de Mogán.

Lineas Salmon (tel: 24 37 08) and *Windjammer San Miguel* (tel: 76 00 76) depart daily from Puerto Rico at 10.30am.

Yellow Submarine (tel: 56 54 96) departs from Puerto de Mogán harbour.

The new marina complex at Puerto de Mogán – all neat and tidy and ship-shape

to make the short boat trip to the golden sands of Puerto Rico (see below).
32km west of Maspalomas.

PUERTO RICO

With its wonderful location in a crescent-shaped bay and long stretches of golden sand, it's no wonder that Puerto Rico is popular. Unfortunately, property development has grown out of control and the surrounding mountainsides are now buried beneath apartment blocks (many of which are empty). The beach cannot possibly support this number of people and is nearly always jam-packed.

The other appeal of Puerto Rico lies in its watersports and fishing facilities. It has the best pleasure harbour on the island, and both its sailing school and its fishing charters enjoy international fame.
18km west of Maspalomas.

SAN NICOLÁS DE TOLENTINO

San Nicolás is a major agricultural centre in a fertile valley. Its great silvery netted greenhouse-like fields are landmarks which can be seen as far away as the centre of the island. The straggling town itself is of no great interest but its port (known as Puerto de la Aldea) is worth a visit for its fish restaurants and the views from its attractive black pebble beach. San Nicolás is also the gateway for the island's most spectacular drive (see pages 46–7).
64km northwest of Maspalomas.

GRAN CANARIA

Route of the Reservoirs Drive

This excursion through the wild interior of the island is as spectacular a route as any on the archipelago, climbing from an altitude of 64m to 1,200m. This is a favourite route for organised jeep safaris but although the road is rough in parts, a four-wheel drive vehicle is not necessary. The narrow, winding roads are often unprotected from steep drops, however, so care and confidence are needed. Don't attempt it in an ordinary car if the weather is poor or it has just rained heavily. The route is just 29km long, but driving conditions are slow. *Allow 2 hours.*

Start in the centre of San Nicolás de Tolentino. Follow the small yellow directional arrow to Artenara (left, right, left).

1 SAN NICOLÁS

The route starts on narrow tracks set amid tall fields of tomatoes and papayas and ramshackle smallholdings. Leaving the fields, the road climbs sharply, following the line of the Barranco de la Aldea, and is very rough. After around 7km it flattens out and becomes smoother. There is a bar and the Embalse (Reservoir) del Caidero to your right. By now the scenery is breathtaking, with peak upon peak rising sharply as far as the eye can see. The valley floor is lush around the reservoirs but the mountains are stark in greys, reds and pinks.

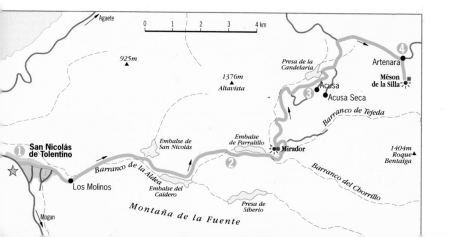

The Parralillo reservoir with Roque Bentaiga in the background

A little further on to the right the Presa de Siberio comes into view (a *presa* is a small reservoir).

The road climbs up to a mirador *(16km past San Nicolás), where the shell of a small windmill, minus its sails, now resembles a sentry box. From here there are wonderful views back down to the Embalse de Parralillo and the Presa de Siberio.*

2 EMBALSE DE PARRALILLO (PARRALILLO RESERVOIR)

This is the most striking of all the reservoirs. If the light is right it will take on a deep, emerald green hue, but in any shade of blue or green it is a fine sight. Across to the east you can see quite clearly the Guanches' sacred rocks of Bentaiga (large and square), and behind it, to the right, Nublo (a smaller, though higher pinnacle) – see pages 28–9.

The road climbs slowly up towards the centre of the island, approaching Roque Bentaiga. After 22km the route reaches the village of Acusa.

3 ACUSA

The Route of the Reservoirs ends in green fields near Acusa, at the Church of La Candelaria. Way down below, to the left, is the last of the reservoirs, the Presa de la Candelaria. (If you would like to

see some cave dwellings take the sign to Acusa.)

Unless you are visiting the caves, keep on the road left to Artenara. Turn right at the Cruz de Acusa crossroads at 26km and after a further 3km you will come to Artenara (see pages 28–9).

4 ARTENARA

To end the trip on a high note, enjoy the magnificent views from the church square or make your way to the Méson de la Silla restaurant (on the road directly above the approach road to the village), where the view is just as spectacular and more beautifully framed.

Caldera de Bandama Walk

The Caldera de Bandama is said to be the most perfectly formed volcanic crater in the Canary Islands. Each year, thousands of coach trippers gaze down into the *caldera* from the (mirador look out point) above – yet very few tourists (or even locals) actually venture down to the valley floor. It's a short but very steep trek to this tiny Shangri-la. Anyone who is moderately fit can do the walk. If it's a nice day take a drink and picnic. *Allow 1½ hours.*

Follow the roadsigns for the Campo de Golf and park as close to the Hotel de Golf as possible.

The views to either side of the road are magnificent. To the *caldera* side you can see the whole of the 1,000m diameter crater opening before you; to the golf club side you can see far beyond the club house and hotel, with the fairways providing carpets of green leading to the distant hills and mountains.

Walk back along the road for half a kilometre until you come to the Restaurant Los Geranios. Go down the short road between restaurant and bus stop and you will come to the steps leading down into the caldera.

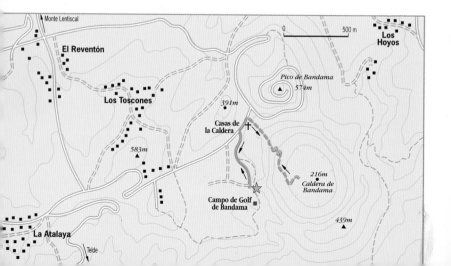

The view from the northern edge of the Caldera de Bandama

After 20 or so large steps the path becomes a narrow dirt track. Don't worry about getting lost – there's just one way, and that's down, 200m to the valley floor. It only takes 15 minutes to make the steep descent but it will take you much longer to get back up.

Towards the bottom of the track you will see, down to the left, the farmhouses where an elderly farmer still lives and works. This path is his only contact with the outside world.

Once on the valley floor, follow the path leading between the drystone walls to the tall, shady eucalyptus trees. In winter the valley floor is a splendid sight, carpeted with bright yellow flowering trefoils, divided neatly by drystone walls and decorated by tall palms and fruit-laden orange trees. The whole scene, complete with its low rustic farmhouses and grazing goats, is more akin to a rather exotic English meadow than an arid Canarian island.

This is effectively the centre of the caldera and the end of the walk. Return by retracing the outward route.

FRAGILE WORLD

The Caldera de Bandama is of great interest to many parties. Guanche caves are located on the sheer, higher levels and may be glimpsed, though only the more adventurous try to explore them. Botanists also come down into the valley to make plant trials in this unique environment. It is a delicate eco-system, however. The coaches which rumble past the crater daily, on their way to the *mirador* above, are ironically damaging the very thing they have come to admire, by causing the side of the crater to slip away (there are plans to re-route heavy vehicles). Walkers should also be sensitive to the environment and stay on the paths of the valley floor, in order to prevent damage to plant-life.

Fuerteventura

*M*iguel de Unamuno, the Spanish poet and philosopher exiled to Fuerteventura by General Franco, once described the island as 'an oasis in the desert of civilisation'. To the less spiritually inclined, however, Fuerteventura is simply a desert, and a windy one at that. In fact it is quite possible that the island took its name from the strong wind, *el viento fuerte*, that is a near-permanent feature here.

Away from the seductive, sandy beaches – the finest in all the Canaries – is a harsh, dusty, arid land, largely devoid of water, trees or people. Fuerteventura is actually the second largest of all the Canary Islands, bigger than Gran Canaria, yet its entire 30,000 population would fit into a small suburb of Las Palmas.

In geological terms, Fuerteventura is the oldest of the islands, and it certainly looks the most ancient. Its once sharp volcanic peaks have been worn and weathered by the elements into a series of gentle humps and bumps, which take on a certain splendour at sunset as they bask and glow in warm, ruddy hues. But it would be wrong to suggest that the landscape of Fuerteventura is dull. Many a visitor finds in it a barren form of grandeur, and the dunes of Corralejo and Jandía are natural wonders of great beauty. Nevertheless, few people come to the island for its sights, or its choice of resorts. The latter are fledglings and all are relatively low-key. Visitors usually come here for quiet beach holidays, or to indulge in some of the best windsurfing conditions in the world, or simply to get away from it all.

Gathering fodder is no easy task on the arid island of Fuerteventura

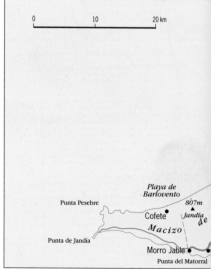

0   10   20 km

Playa de Barlovento

Punta Pesebre

Cofete   807m
Jandía
Macizo *de*

Punta de Jandía

Morro Jable
Punta del Matorral

FUERTEVENTURA

Punta de la Tiñosa

Isla de los Lobos

Majanicho

Corralejo

El Río

Punta de la Ballena

157m
▲
*Calderón
Hondo*

*Playas de
Corralejo*

Cotillo

Lajares

El Jable

Playa del Algibe de la Cueva

Taca

**Centro de
Arte Canario** ■

La Oliva ■ ■ **Casa de los Coroneles**

Caldereta

Tindaya

Vallebrón

**Monumento a
D Miguel
de Unamuno** ■

■ La Matilla

Los Molinos

Tefía

Tetir

**PUERTO
DEL ROSARIO** ■

Loma de Salinas

Casillas
del Angel

Playa Blanca
Parador Nacional ■

Llanos de la
Concepcion

Playa Blanca ●

**Catedral
Santa María** ■ ■ **Ruinas del
Convento**

● Triquivijate

✈

Playa del Matorral

Betancuria

Antigua

Puerto de la Peña ●

Ermita de la Peña

Vega del Río
de Palmas ●

708m
▲
*Gran
Montaña*

Casilla
de Morales

Caleta de Fustes ●
■ **Castillo de Fustes**

Playa del Castillo

Ruinas Guanches ●
● La Torre

606m
▲
Carbón

● Pájara

● Tuineje

*Malpaís
Grande*

Puerto Pozo Negro ●
Playa Pozo Negro

Llano del Sombrerito

**Ruinas
Guanches**

Teseyerague ●

Punta de las Borriquillas

*Playa de
la Pared*

Peñon del Roque
● Las Playitas

Gran Tarajal ●

Tarajalejo ●

● La Lajita

Matas Blancas ●

● Costa Calma

Playa Esmeralda Jandía

Jandía

*Playa de
Sotavento*

Jandía Playa

Central Fuerteventura

*B*etween the beaches of north and south is a bare, arid, gently undulating volcanic landscape. A drive to Betancuria, the island's historical and literal oasis, is a must, and there is enough sightseeing here for a leisurely day out.

ANTIGUA

Although Antigua dates back to 1485 it's an unremarkable place, redeemed only by a handsome 18th-century church which contains a venerated image and has a pretty garden.

Just to the north is a fine stone windmill, beautifully restored to its pristine condition of some 200 years ago. The adjacent fine granary building has been converted into a popular rustic restaurant. An *artesanía* (craft workshop) is currently being built next door.
46km south of Corralejo.

BETANCURIA

The island conqueror, Jean de Béthencourt, founded his capital here in 1405, away from the coast, to escape Berber pirate attacks. It enjoys a picturesque location, alongside a dry river bed in a valley which remains fertile on account of its high water table. Unfortunately, the Berbers were undeterred by the long trek inland, and in 1539 destroyed the church (also known as the Cathedral of Santa María) and shipped off 600 Christians to slavery. Rebuilt in 1620, the church has quite a plain interior with naïve-style pastel-painted side altars providing relief from the baroque high altar. Don't miss the Judgement Day painting in the

The ancient capital of Betancuria is a welcome oasis in the dusty interior

southwest chapel. The Church Museum, Museo de Arte Sacro, is housed in the ancient former presbytery across the church square. Within its four rooms, the most important treasures are the figure of Santiago (see San Bartolomé de Tirajana, page 41) and the *Pendón de la Conquista* (Banner of the Conquest), thought to be Béthencourt's original flag.

Betancuria continued to be the island capital until 1834 but today the settlement is little more than a village. Some of its ancient houses date back over five centuries. There is a low-key archaeology museum (Museo Arqueológico) on the other side of the river, where you will also find shops and a local bar-restaurant.

Five minutes' walk north of town (accessible from the main road, but easy to miss) are the picturesque ruins of a Franciscan Convent, (Ruinas del Convento) built in 1414.

48km south of Corralejo. Only one person tends the church and the Museo de Arte Sacro, therefore opening times alternate on each half hour and last for half an hour: Open: Monday to Friday, 10.30am–1.30pm and 3pm–4.30pm; Saturday, 10.30am–1.30pm and mass (church only) at 5pm.

CASTILLO/CALETA DE FUSTES

This pleasant, if rather characterless new low-rise seaside development is based around a golden beach and culminates in a small pleasure marina with a modern lighthouse building. Fishing charters and a diving school operate from here. The eponymous castle is a small circular 18th-century tower, incorporated pleasantly into a plaza with shops and a swimming pool.

10km south of airport. The castle is not open to the public.

The windmill at La Antigua is indicative of the island's notorious wind, *el viento fuerte*

PÁJARA

This bright and tidy small village is famous for its church Iglesia de la Virgen de la Regla which dates from 1645–87. Its wooden altars are decorated with simply painted flowers, and there is a coffered ceiling (100-peseta coins operate the lights). However, it is the church portal which is remarkable – made of soft, pink sandstone and carved with Aztec-style symbols of suns and snakes, lions and doves. It is thought to date from the 16th century, but its origin is a mystery.

15km south of Betancuria.

VEGA DEL RÍO DE PALMAS

The literal translation, 'Valley of the River of Palms', spells out the scenic attraction of this oasis area. The Santuario Virgen de la Peña is an atmospheric old church with a statue of the Virgin and a 14th-century confessional. Note the large number of 1920s Aeromotor Chicago Co windpumps still operating around here.

5km south of Betancuria. Church open: Tuesday to Sunday, 11am–1pm and 5pm–7pm.

Northern Fuerteventura

Northern Fuerteventura is a fine place for a family holiday. Corralejo offers most facilities, including fabulous dunes, the chance to visit a real desert island and a day excursion to Lanzarote. For culture vultures, the excellent modern art gallery at La Oliva and the historic charms of Betancuria (see pages 52–3) are within easy reach.

CORRALEJO

This is the most complete resort on the island, yet still manages to retain a local atmosphere. It clusters around the fishing port, with ferries plying to and from Lanzarote (40 minutes) and Isla de los Lobos (see below), while children play on the small sandy beaches. The centre is a small, busy square with a bandstand, shops and tourist restaurants. Just around the corner are the locals' bars and restaurants. The 10km-long snow-white beach and dunes, for which Corralejo is famous, lie just outside town. The dunes, set against a rugged mountain backdrop, are wild and beautiful.

38km north of the airport.

The fishing fleet of El Cotillo

COTILLO

Cotillo is a small, dusty fishing village on the west coast with a handful of holiday apartments and a couple of restaurants. It has a certain 'frontier' appeal; there is a beach to the north of the harbour, colonised by new houses and apartments, but the best sands lie a short distance south (on unmade roads), past the 17th-century tower of Castillo de Rico Roque (not open to the public). Beware of off-shore winds if swimming from either beaches.

22km southwest of Corralejo.

ISLA DE LOS LOBOS

Los Lobos refers to the seals (*lobos marinos*) which once swam off this tiny island. A good beach, a drinks shack, natural beauty and peace and quiet are its simple but alluring ingredients.

Glass-bottom boats make the trip to the island so that the clear waters may be enjoyed en route.

3km (30-minute) boat trip north of Corralejo. Trips depart from Corralejo harbour at 10am daily and return from Los Lobos at 4pm daily. Book through any local travel agent.

LA OLIVA

During the 18th century this village was the joint seat of government with Antigua. Since then it has fallen on hard times. Its stagnation is summed up by the grandiose, decaying Casa de los

Coroneles (House of the Colonels). This 18th-century, 40-room mansion, with fine Canarian balconies, was the house of the islands' military commanders, and was used up until the middle of this century by Franco's forces.

Another haughty building (also closed to the public) is the parish church, which holds some fine paintings, but is currently undergoing lengthy restoration work. Very definitely open is the new Centro de Arte Canario, one of the finest collections of modern Canarian art on the islands. Works range from completely avant-garde to completely accessible and are well displayed in traditional and modern settings.
La Oliva is 16km south of Corralejo. Centro de Arte Canario (tel: 86 82 33). Open: Monday to Saturday, summer 10am–6pm, winter 10am–5pm. Admission charge.

PUERTO DEL ROSARIO

Despite its capital status, there's nothing in this town of interest to tourists. Still, you could do worse than browse around the small, tourism-free centre, then enjoy a plate of *el cocido* (the island's meat and

The House of the Colonels, La Oliva

chickpea stew) in one of the cafés overlooking the harbour. Ferries run from here to Lanzarote.
30km south of Corralejo. Tourist Information: Cabildo Insular building (side door), Avenida 1 de Mayo 33 (tel: 85 10 24). Open: Monday to Friday, 7.45am–3.30pm.

A beach of your own – near Corralejo

THE SPANISH FOREIGN LEGION
While Spain still clings onto her North African territories of Ceuta and Melilla, it's likely that Fuerteventura, the nearest Canarian territory to Africa, will remain the base for that most hard-bitten of all its armed forces – the Spanish Foreign Legion. Their headquarters is in Puerto del Rosario, on the Corralejo road next to the port. Here, in formal gardens in front of the barracks, is a display of modern weaponry, heroic statues and some curious wooden totem poles.

Southern Fuerteventura

The south of Fuerteventura can only mean the magnificent beaches of the Jandía peninsula. Along with those of Corralejo they are rated the best in all the Canaries.

GRAN TARAJAL/TARAJALEJO

Gran Tarajal is the port from which Fuerteventura's high-grade tomatoes are shipped. Next to the port is a black beach with a smart new promenade and a handful of cafés and restaurants. The former fishing village of Tarajalejo, a few kilometres along the coast, has a similar black beach and resort aspirations. But with the golden sands of Jandía just a short drive south, it's unlikely that either of these resorts will expand beyond a local clientèle.

Gran Tarajal and Tarajalejo are 53km and 40km, respectively, northeast of Morro Jable.

JANDÍA

The Playa de Sotavento ('leeward beach') which lines the whole south coast of the Jandía peninsula is the beach which has made Fuerteventura famous. These golden white shores, lapped by ultramarine waters, have launched a thousand postcards and attract the bulk of the island's tourists. There are over 30km to choose from, so it's not difficult to find a patch of your own. The beach varies from pretty coves with low-cliff backing (as at Costa Calma) to magnificent dunes (just south of the landmark Hotel Los Gorriones) to great desert-like expanses. This coast is world famous as a windsurfing venue (see pages 58–9).

The development along here is mostly uninspiring – boxes of whitewashed *urbanizaciones* climb up the hills and *centro commerciales* provide bland ersatz-village centres.

The northernmost point of the Jandía peninsula, Casas de Matas Blancas, is several kilometres southwest of the airport.

LAS PLAYITAS

Authentic fishing villages are a novelty on Fuerteventura, so it's worth a detour to this attractive little spot, which has been colonised to a lesser extent by a clutch of apartments and bungalows. There's a good (dark) beach and some highly regarded fish restaurants.

6.5km northeast of Gran Tarajal.

MORRO JABLE

This is the southernmost resort of the Jandía peninsula and the only settlement of any character on this coast. It is built on either side of a *barranco* (ravine), and its erstwhile existence as a fishing village just manages to survive the tourist invasion (the worst excesses of this are to the east, in the new resort of Jandía Playa). There's a pleasant promenade by the town beach, with a choice of cafés and restaurants.

Unless you have a four-wheel drive vehicle, this is the end of the line. The road south goes no further.

A hydrofoil service links Morro Jable to Tenerife.

Southeast of the airport.

PLAYA DE BARLOVENTO

This wild beach (its name means 'windward') on the north coast of the

Rhapsody in Blue – the breathtaking shoreline of Playa de Sotavento, on the Jandía peninsula

Jandía peninsula is only accessible to four-wheel drive vehicles. Those who do make the effort are rewarded with superb, unspoiled scenery. It's a glorious beach but most certainly not a place for swimming. The currents here are treacherous and have claimed the lives of several unwary tourists in recent years. The only sign of civilisation is the bar and hamlet of Cofete. From here you can see the large, derelict Villa Winter. Gustav Winter, a German engineer, was given this land by General Franco for services rendered. Winter was also a Nazi sympathiser and it is rumoured that this was a half-way house for war criminals fleeing to South America.

8km north of Jandía.

WIND SURFING

Windsurfing is by far the most popular watersport in the Canaries and the beaches of Sotavento (Jandía, Fuerteventura) and El Médano (Tenerife) draw devotees of the sport from all over the world. The winds don't *always* blow on the islands, however, and the average reliability rate is around 50 per cent in winter and 60–75 per cent in summer. Tenerife is windier than Lanzarote, which is windier than Fuerteventura. However, when it comes to wave-sailing conditions, the order is probably reversed.

The annual world championship speed finals are held at Playa de Sotavento in August and, with wind speeds up to force 9, contestants fly across the waves. International Speed Weeks are also held here. The centre of activity is the Procenter F2 school at Los Gorriones hotel.

On the windward (western) side of Fuerteventura conditions can also be thrilling and Cotillo is a popular spot with experienced windsurfers, but beware – this beach is said to break more kit than any other surf location in Europe! The west side of the island should be treated with great caution, due to treacherous currents.

El Médano, on the east coast of Tenerife, is generally very windy indeed and is the venue for the World Cup each July. There are two F2 centres here. Playa de las Américas also provides some thrilling and heavy wave-sailing conditions.

On Gran Canaria, speed merchants are well catered for at Maspalomas/ Playa del Inglés, where four-times world champion Björn Dunkerbeck directs the Passat School. Come in

When the going gets tough, the tough get going – cutting the water at El Médano, on Tenerife's east coast

summer, when the southerly tradewinds provide extremely fast conditions.

The Lanzarote Surf Company, at Costa Teguise, is another F2 centre where the surfing reaches epic speeds. Experienced sailors may also like to check out Famara (not for the faint-hearted!) and Jameos del Agua.

It's not all thrills and spills, however. If you are just learning, or progressing, there are several venues throughout the larger islands which provide experienced tuition and calm waters on which to build up confidence and perfect technique (see **Sport**). Take all the usual precautions and bear in mind that there are very few rescue services.

El Sendero de Bayuyo Walk

This walk follows an ancient pathway (*sendero*), recently renovated by the island tourism authorities to show something of the volcanic origins and wild landscape of Fuerteventura. An interpretive centre is planned, and its site is marked half-way along the walk. This is an easy trek for all ages and fitness levels and until it is nearer completion, most of it can be negotiated by four-wheel drive vehicle. If you can time the walk for sunset you will enjoy the wonderful sight of the landscape bathed in rich velvety reds, browns and purples. Out of the sun, however, you may need to wrap up (particularly in winter). *Allow 1½ hours.*

To find the Sendero de Bayuyo, turn off the Lajares road by the Campo de Futbol, continue for exactly 1km and the start of the path is clearly marked, next to a house, on the right.

The walk initially heads straight for the Montaña Colorada (Coloured Mountain), an ancient volcano of many hues, then

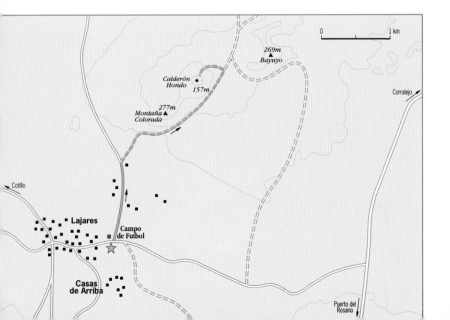

Ancient enclosures, walls and paths criss-cross the landscape beneath the Calderón Hondo

skirts it to the right. Notice the low stone walls which divide apparently empty fields; even in this arid wilderness crops are grown.

The path climbs slowly, with the wind in your face, skirting an adjacent volcano, Calderón Hondo. The views backwards (south), to the the side (east) and forwards (north) sweep across miles of empty countryside, bordered by ancient, softly rounded volcanic cones. After 20 minutes you will see the great golden-white beach of Corralejo ahead of you in the distance. After a few more minutes the Isla de los Lobos (to the right) and Lanzarote (in the far distance) become clear.

Take the fork to the left and after around 30 minutes the path ascends to the top of the volcano.

Here, 223m above Corralejo, there is a viewing platform (and safety rails) for looking down into the 8,000-year-old crater. The golden beaches of Playa Blanca and volcanic landscape of Lanzarote are also clearly visible. *Descend the path and continue down to the left.*

Disappointingly, the path ends in a small, scrubby, sandy area. If you have proper walking gear and you are feeling adventurous it is possible to walk right round the volcanoes. If not, simply return along the same path.

A VOLCANIC EXTENSION

The Path of Bayuyo is part of an old trail which connects Corralejo to the interior. All of this land was created some 8,000 years ago in a series of volcanic eruptions which formed the present northern coast of the island and also threw up the island of Los Lobos. If you want to continue to Corralejo, take the path leading down to the sea (this soon peters out, so sturdy walking shoes are advisable), visible from Calderón Hondo. The last volcano before Corralejo is Bayuyo, at 269m the highest of the group. It's an easy climb and offers the best views north. Allow three hours' walking to get to Corralejo; then it's a short taxi ride (about 10km) back to the start of the route.

Lanzarote

*I*n any poll of favourite Canary Islands, Lanzarote will always come near the top. This extraordinary place is, above all, visually striking. Many volcanic islands around the world have black beaches and some have blackened fields, yet none has turned a volcanic catastrophe into such an art form.

LANZAROTE

In back gardens the black ash has been corralled as neatly as any manicured lawn, surrounded by whitewashed stone walls and planted with hibiscus and bougainvillea. The houses are small and white, with green frames and doors (the island's official colour scheme), and their chimneys are topped with Moorish-style onion domes. In the fields, potatoes, onions and tomatoes grow under the same volcanic debris. Each group of plants is protected from sun and wind by a semi-circular stone wall. As this repeating pattern slopes away to infinity against the blackened mountain slopes, the effect is as hypnotic as any piece of modern art. To add to this are the beautiful beaches of the south and the unpolluted azure seas around the island.

Lanzaroteños have long realised the value of their landscape and in order to preserve it they have banned all visual distractions. Thus there are no disfiguring advertising hoardings, no pylons (cables run underground) and no high-rise blocks to blot the surroundings.

The man largely responsible for these environmental measures was island hero César Manrique (1919–92). This multi-talented artist and designer also created a series of semi-natural attractions on the island that no visitor should miss.

For all the island's neat and tidy ways, however, the visitor's abiding memory will be of a chaos that no man could have created or mastered. Lanzarote's Mountains of Fire are as convincing a lunar landscape as any on earth and the ultimate visual thrill on this unique island.

The Mirador del Río offers one of the Canaries' most spectacular views

Arrecife and Puerto del Carmen

*T*he only thing that Arrecife and Puerto del Carmen have in common is that they were once small fishing ports. Nowadays Arrecife is Lanzarote's principal town, while Puerto del Carmen is the principal resort. Neither is large; half the island's total population may live in Arrecife, but that is only 40,000 people, and Puerto del Carmen, though expanding, is still far from becoming the next Playa de las Américas. The most charming parts of each are to be found, inevitably, where the fishing boats lie.

ARRECIFE

For the capital of such a fascinating island, Arrecife is a disappointment. Its streets are dusty and potholed, its architecture modern and characterless, and a mazy one-way system tests drivers' navigational skills to the limit. The main attraction is the late 18th-century Castillo de San José, restored to hold the acclaimed Museo Internacional de Arte Contemporáneo (International Museum of Contemporary Art), which includes works by Picasso and Miró. This lies a short distance out of town, just off the Costa Teguise road.

The castle on a small island, just off

the seafront near the centre of town, is the Castillo de San Gabriel, built in 1590. This now houses a small archaeological museum. The landmark church tower opposite the castle belongs to the Iglesia de San Ginés, recently restored to its 18th-century glory and well worth a visit. Behind it is the capital's most charming spot, El Charco San Ginés (the lagoon of San Ginés), where small boats gently bob at anchor. There is a promenade around the lagoon and a handful of bars and restaurants. Bigger boats lie north of here – Arrecife is the island's main fishing port. There is also a ferry service to Fuerteventura and Gran Canaria.

6km east of the airport. Tourist Information: Avenida Generalisimo Franco (seafront) (tel: 81 18 60). Open: Monday to Friday, 10am–2pm and 4.30–7pm; Saturday, 10am–2pm. Castillo de San José, Avenida de Naos (tel: 81 10 60). Open: daily, 11am–9pm. Admission free. Castello de San Gabriel museum (tel: 81 19 50). Open: Monday to Friday, 8am–2pm. Admission free. Iglesia de San Ginés, Plaza de San Ginés, off Aquilino Fernández. Open: services only.

Built on the orders of King Philip II of Spain, the Castillo de San José protects Arrecife's deep-water fishing harbour

Puerto del Carmen's old port is a picturesque and lively place

FUNDACIÓN CÉSAR MANRIQUE
(César Manrique Foundation)

This was the home and studio of the late great Lanzarote artist (see pages 66–7) until 1987 and it was opened to the public in 1992, a few months after his death. Here you can see some of his best works of art and get a preview of the attractions that he has designed on the island. His house is a startling troglodyte vision, though these caves are not man-made, but the result of five volcanic gas bubbles. The landscaping here is a rehearsal for his Jameos del Agua masterpiece (see pages 70–1). The Foundation has a bookshop, souvenir boutique, snack bar and parking.
Tahíche, 5km north of Arrecife (tel: 81 01 38 or 81 42 70). Open: daily, 10am–7pm. Admission charge.

PUERTO DEL CARMEN

This is by far the island's largest and busiest resort, stretching some 5km along a golden beach, which gets better as it heads south. The front is heavily commercialised and the César Manrique spirit is lost amid gaudy bars and restaurant fronts. A few metres back, however, peace and quiet return, amid developments which are low-rise, painted green and white and surrounded by pretty gardens.

The old part of town survives around the picturesque fishing port. This is a charming, small area of good fish restaurants and down-to-earth bars where old sea-dogs and tourists rub shoulders. In the square next to the port you can watch the locals playing *boules.*

For boats of an altogether smarter variety, head south for 8km to the pretty new development of Puerto Calero, where a pleasure marina is being established in a small bay.
Puerto del Carmen old town is 10km south-west of the airport. Tourist Information: Avenida del Playas (seafront, opposite Restaurante Playa Mar) (no telephone). Open: Monday to Friday, 10am–2pm and 4pm–7pm; Saturday, 10am–2pm.

CÉSAR MANRIQUE

The tribute most often paid to César Manrique is that without his efforts tourist development on Lanzarote would have followed the high-rise, high-density route and the island would have lost its identity. In the environmentally conscious 1990s Lanzarote is studied by other countries who are developing tourism, and is used as a role model.

Manrique was born in Arrecife in 1919 and studied art in Madrid and New York, at a time when surrealism was a major influence. He returned to his beloved island in 1968 and determined to preserve its natural beauty in the face of tourism. His major set-piece visitor attractions, Jameos del Agua (bottom left), Mirador del Río and Jardín de Cactus (top left) (see pages 70–1) are masterpieces of design which are totally in harmony with the landscape.

The hallmarks of any Manrique project are the use of local materials, integration with nature and a completely peaceful atmosphere (often helped by ethereal 'mood music'), all finished with a flourish of his own brand of surreal art.

Manrique was far more than just an artist and designer, however. He was the driving force behind the island's whole tourism development philosophy. He was a fiery orator and a tireless promoter of the island, and it is thanks to him that almost all the architecture on Lanzarote is in traditional style, and that there is still a total ban on advertising hoardings.

César Manrique died in a car accident just outside his Taro de Tahíche home in September 1992. His influence has been so pervasive throughout Lanzarote that his philosophy is sure to live on.

THE MANRIQUE ROLL CALL
In addition to the projects listed
above, César Manrique also designed
the following island attractions:
Monumento al Campesino, Mozaga;
Fundación César Manrique (above
and left), Tahíche; Restaurant El
Diablo and the devil-motif park
boundary signs, Montañas del Fuego;
Museo Internacional del Arte
Contemporáneo, Arrecife; Las Salinas
hotel, Costa Teguise; La Era
restaurant, Yaiza (conversion and
restoration). Look out, too, for his
weird and wonderful wind-mobiles
around the island.

   Manrique's talents are also in
evidence on other Canary Islands:
Lido Martiánez and Playa Jardín in
Puerto de la Cruz, on Tenerife;
Mirador de la Peña on El Hierro;
Mirador del Palmarejo (still under
construction) on La Gomera;
Restaurant El Molino near Antigua, on
Fuerteventura.

The many creations of Manrique – from
landscape design to modern sculpture

Montañas del Fuego

*L*anzarote's Montañas del Fuego ('Mountains of Fire') is one of the most dramatic landscapes on earth. In fact, the Earth will probably be the farthest place from your mind as you view this apocalyptic scene. The brooding craters and scorched, pock-marked land are completely lunar in appearance. Yet even within these badlands, the locals harvest crops, and on the very edge of the Mountains of Fire, vineyards flourish.

EL GOLFO

The main attraction at El Golfo ('the Gulf') is a small lagoon which, when the light is right, glows a deep emerald green, caused by its algae. Surrounding this is half of the old volcano of El Golfo; the other half has been eaten away by the sea to create a spectacular amphitheatre with a richly coloured cross-section.

The lagoon is not obvious from the main road. Just before you enter the small fishing village of El Golfo (famous for its restaurants), park your car on the hill to the left and walk the short way around the headland to find it.
12km northwest of Yaiza.

LA GERIA

La Geria is a valley of black volcanic ash which has been ingeniously cultivated to become Lanzarote's wine region. Vines are planted in shallow depressions, each surrounded by a horse-shoe shaped stone wall, about a metre high. This gives protection from the wind and helps the lava covering the crop (see pages 72–3) condense what little moisture there is. The effect of thousands of these shelters, stretching across the coal-black hillsides, is as startling as any piece of modern art.

The Mountains of Fire – still aglow after 260 years of activity

Ingenious methods of cultivation draw crops from the ashes at La Geria. Low stone walls protect individual plants from the srong prevailing winds

And despite the apparently barren condition each vine can produce up to 200kg of grapes. You can taste the end product at any one of several *bodegas* (wineries), signposted off the Masdache-Uga road, which follows the valley and delineates the region.

PARQUE NACIONAL DE TIMANFAYA/MONTAÑAS DEL FUEGO

The Mountains of Fire were largely created between 1730 and 1736 by a series of 26 volcanic eruptions which devastated around a quarter of the island and buried 11 villages. Fortunately there were no casualties, but many *Lanzaroteños* lost everything and were forced to emigrate to Gran Canaria. In 1974 the area around the epicentre of this region was declared the National Park of Timanfaya (named after the largest of the volcanoes).

If you approach from the south, the badlands of the Mountains of Fire start just north of Yaiza. You are not allowed to leave your car in this area; it is impossible to walk on the devastated terrain, anyway. Stop at the Echadero de los Camellos ('Camel Park') and you can ride on a dromedary into the volcanic wasteland. The activity here is sometimes frenetic and well worth seeing, though the 10–15-minute ride is really only of novelty value.

A little further on, a ticket kiosk gives access to the Islote de Hilario, which is as far into the park as cars are permitted. Here, a guide demonstrates the geotherm-al energy below your feet: a tube of water is transformed into a scalding geyser and a dry bush ignites when dropped into a crevice. A restaurant here uses the volcano as a giant barbecue.

Included in your ticket price is the 'Route of the Volcanoes' coach tour. This is an unforgettable 1-hour tour, with commentary, including a stop at a breath-taking *mirador* right above the fissure line. (If you do this tour as part of a travel package it may not stop at the *mirador* – check before you book.)

For details of a guided walk in the Mountains of Fire see pages 78–9. *National Park entrance is 7km north of Yaiza (tel: 84 00 57). Open: daily, 9am–4.45pm (last coach tour). Admission charge. Camel Park is 3km north of Yaiza. Open: daily, 9am–4/5pm.*

Northern Lanzarote

*T*he north of Lanzarote was unscathed by the 18th-century volcanic devastation of Timanfaya and so has a less scarred character than the south. Nevertheless, the northern massif is spectacular, and César Manrique (see page 17) has enhanced nature with three outstanding creations.

CUEVA DE LOS VERDES

The 'Greens' Cave' (which takes its name from previous owners) was created some 5,000 years ago by exploding volcanic gases and lava creating a labyrinth of tunnels from Monte Corona to the sea. These total some 7km and once provided a refuge from pirates. Nowadays guides take tourists along 2km of the tunnels, ducking and dodging along narrow, often low, atmospherically lit passageways. A memorable trip ends with a brilliant natural optical illusion.
26km north of Arrecife (tel: 83 50 10). Open: daily, 10am–6pm (last tour 5pm). Admission charge.

The labyrinthine Cueva de los Verdes

HARÍA

Haría is a pristine white village set in the middle of a beautiful, palm-studded valley. Do look in at the Centro Artesanía handicraft centre and El Museo Sacro Popular (the Museum of

Sacred Popular Art).

The best view of the village and valley is to be had from the Mirador de Haría, 4km south. From here it resembles a North African oasis settlement.

Some 4km north is the Guinate Tropical Bird Park, set on the cliffside. About 300 species are represented here and parrot shows delight the children. *Haría is 15km northeast of Teguise. Centro Artesanía, Calle Barranco, 4. Closed lunchtime, Monday afternoon and Sunday morning. Museo de Arte Sacro (tel: 83 50 09) is adjacent to Iglesia de la Encarnacion. Open: Monday to Friday, 11am–1pm and 4pm–6pm. Admission charge. Guinate Tropical Bird Park (tel: 83 55 00). Open: daily, 10am–5pm. Admission charge.*

ISLA GRACIOSA

This small island is just 2km from Lanzarote at its nearest point. There are no cars and no tourist developments – just excellent beaches, a bar-restaurant and a couple of *pensions* (see pages 136–7).
40-minute daily ferry service from Orzola (35km north of Arrecife). Departs 10am, returns 4pm.

JAMEOS DEL AGUA

A *jameo* is a subterranean chamber or cave, formed by a volcanic gas bubble, which has lost its roof and is open to the air. This spectacular creation uses a series of these chambers to create a fantasy grotto. The first is transformed into a cool restaurant-bar area, luxuriant with tropical plants. A shallow mirror pool leads to a tiny underground lagoon. Peer into the darkness and you will see tiny white albino crabs, usually only found deep in the ocean, and stranded here long ago. As you emerge from the darkness there's a shock in store: an idyllic South Seas beach vision with a tall palm bending over bright blue water. Yet another cave is used in the evenings for folk dancing and other entertainments. *27km north of Arrecife (tel: 85 50 10). Open: daily, 11am–7pm; Tuesday and Saturday, also 7pm–3am (higher entrance charge for these times). Admission charge.*

JARDÍN DE CACTUS (Cactus Garden)

Don't be put off by the dry-sounding concept of a cactus garden. This is an inspired piece of landscaping with over 10,000 specimens of all shapes and sizes, interspersed with huge finger-shaped volcanic rocks, reminiscent of a Dalí painting. The centrepiece is a beautifully preserved windmill which still grinds *gofio* (see page 162).
Guatiza, 17km northeast of Arrecife (tel: 52 93 97). Open: daily, 9.30am–6pm. Admission charge.

Above: salt pans of sea water at El Rio
Below: the Plaza de la Constitucion, Haría

MIRADOR DEL RÍO

This ancient lookout point is one of the finest *miradores* in all the Canary Islands. It was once used to warn of approaching pirate ships and in the 1898 Spanish-American war was a gun battery. César Manrique added curving white walls, picture windows, a balcony, a restaurant and a bar. From a height of 450m it descends in an almost sheer drop to reveal the beautiful beaches of Graciosa, the striking blue strait of El Río, and little pink and grey salt pan squares – the sort of 'natural modern art' in which Manrique delighted.
9km north of Haría (tel: (908) 64 43 18). Open: daily, 10am–6pm. Admission charge.

ISLAND AGRICULTURE

their surprise and delight when their crops not only began to grow through the cinders, but were actually healthier than before. The *Lanzaroteños* soon learned that the porous black *lapilli* or *picon* (pumice particles) helped to soak up what little moisture was in the air, particularly at dusk, and so nourished their plants. This knowledge was passed to the other dry islands and the spreading of *lapilli* became a common agricultural method on Fuerteventura. Lanzarote's main crops are potatoes, onions and tomatoes, but vines are also important.

Lanzarote is also still home to the cochineal industry, albeit now on a very minor scale compared with its heyday in the 19th century. Cochineal bugs are raised on prickly pear cacti (originally imported from Mexico), then dried and crushed for the bright red dye, which

L ife on the land has always been particularly hard on the eastern Canary Islands. If the sun does not burn the crops and the wind does not blow them away, a freak gust of locusts, blown across from North Africa, can devour a season's work in minutes. Imagine, then, the feelings of Lanzarote's farmers, surveying their fields, covered by a layer of black volcanic ash, following the devastating explosions of the 1730s. Imagine, too,

Eking an existence from the land in Fuerteventura and Lanzarote

among other uses goes to colour aperitifs such as Campari. César Manrique's Jardín de Cactus (see pages 70–1), constructed in the cochineal/cactus growing area of Guatiza, is as much of a tribute to Lanzarote's cochineal farmers as his Monumento al Campesino (see pages 76–7) is to all Lanzarote's field workers.

On the other islands, bananas have been the main crop since the cochineal demise, yet these too are in decline. Most European buyers reject the small Canarian bananas (Spain takes over 90 per cent of the crop) and there was even speculation recently that the EU would fail to recognise them as bananas! Exotic fruits, such as papayas and avocados, and cut flowers are now beginning to replace some banana fields as farmers diversify, but acre upon acre of dark green plantations are still the major feature on the northern coasts of Gran Canaria and the western islands.

Southern Lanzarote

*T*he southern peninsula of Lanzarote is topographically the least interesting part of the island. However, for those who brave the rough, unsigned tracks beyond Playa Blanca, the prize is some of the best beaches in the archipelago.

FEMÉS

This small hamlet is perched on a spectacularly sited saddle between the mountains overlooking Playa Blanca, and is by far the most scenic way to approach the beaches. Stop here on your way back, too, to watch the sun set, colouring the Mountains of Fire in dusky reds and purples. The church of Femés is one of the oldest on the island.
8km northeast of Playa Blanca.

PLAYA BLANCA

The old fishing village of Playa Blanca has been submerged under a new resort which is still far short of completion. There are two main centres of activity. The largest and more mature is just east of the Fuerteventura ferry terminal. A pleasant promenade with bars and restaurants overlooks the main town beach. There is another, smaller, though no less pleasant beach, on the other side of the port, known as Playa Flamingo. Both of these beaches soon become full, however, encouraging sun-worshippers to head for Playa Blanca's famous Papagayo ('parrot') beaches. These begin 5km to the east of the resort and comprise three distinct beaches: Playa de Mujeres, Playa Papagayo and Puerto Muelas (also known as La Caleta).

There is one sign to these golden sands and then the asphalt road

Large-scale commercial saltpans at Janubio

The almost clinical neatness of the houses of Yaiza, whitewashed to repel the heat of the sun

disintegrates into a maze of bumpy, dusty dirt tracks. Carloads of people looking puzzled, frustrated and simply driving in circles are a common sight just east of Playa Blanca! Many park by the landmark round tower of Castillo de las Coloradas (built in 1769) and make the 25-minute walk to Playa de Mujeres. The only foolproof method of driving all the way there is to follow someone who knows the way – which is not difficult, as these beaches are very popular.

Having arrived, you will find golden sandy coves with picturesque cliff backings. Playa Papagayo is prettiest of all and is the only one with a bar-restaurant, though itinerant drinks vendors service the other beaches. Puerto Muelas is popular with nudists.
Playa Blanca is 35km southwest of the airport.

SALINAS DE JANUBIO

The saltpans (or saltflats) of Janubio is one of the island's oldest industries, producing salt for the fish processing plants of Arrecife. On a bright day the chequer-board effect of the individual pans, where the seawater evaporates to leave gleaming white squares, is yet

another of the island's natural art works. A natural spectacle of a different kind is provided 3km north by Los Hervideros ('the boiling springs') where, in rough weather, waves break violently and spout up through volcanic sea caves.
Salinas de Janubio is 9km north of Playa Blanca.

YAIZA

Yaiza is usually regarded as the prettiest village on Lanzarote – a neat and tidy collection of old whitewashed houses with charming floral gardens. The most popular place in the village, the Restaurant La Era, contains one of only three houses which were left standing in Yaiza after the cataclysmic events of 1730–6 (see page 69). César Manrique (see pages 66–7) renovated the house, extended it and converted it into a restaurant in 1970. Do have a look in, whether or not you intend dining (there is a separate bar area). Also in Yaiza is a fine old 18th-century church, a good private art gallery and a Casa de Cultura (Cultural Centre), which also provides art exhibition space (but does not keep to its stated opening hours).
15km north of Playa Blanca.

Teguise

The town of Teguise is the historic showcase of Lanzarote, with many fine examples of colonial architecture. But life for the island's peasants was (and still is) hard. This is well illustrated by some of the other visitor attractions in this area.

CASA MUSEO/MONUMENTO AL CAMPESINO (Museum/Monument to the Field Worker)

César Manrique's tribute to Lanzarote's long-suffering farmers takes the surreal shape of a 15m high glistening, white tower of blocks which is said to represent the farmer, his cat and a rat. Symbolically, it is placed in the exact centre of the island. Next to it, Manrique designed a traditional farmhouse which holds a restaurant, a small museum (where artisans often give craft demonstrations) and a shop selling local produce.

Mozaga, 8km northwest of Arrecife (tel: 52 01 36). Open: daily, 10am–6pm. Admission free.

CASTILLO DE SANTA BÁRBARA

High on the old volcano of Guanapay, this golden-coloured castle was built in the 16th century to protect the people of Teguise against pirates. Today it houses the Museo del Emigrante Canario (Museum of the Canarian Emigrant), which relates the sad history of mass emigration by Canarian families to South America. The views from here are superb.

1km northeast of Teguise (tel: 81 19 50). Open: Tuesday to Sunday, 10am–3pm. Admission charge.

COSTA TEGUISE

This large, new up-market *urbanización* (development) is built around an excellent sandy beach. Watersport facilities are good and there is an 18-hole golf course and aquapark on site. *7km northeast of Arrecife.*

TEGUISE

Teguise is the oldest town on the island, founded in the 15th century, and was the capital until 1852. There are dozens of

The main square and the ancient church of historic Teguise

old buildings to admire, many beautifully restored, in a peaceful atmosphere which cloaks the town six days of the week. On Sunday pandemonium breaks out as half the island population and most of its tourists descend on the Sunday market (see pages 142–3).

The main square is dominated by the great bulk of the Iglesia de Nuestra Señora de Guadalupe (Church of Our Lady of Guadalupe), also known as the Iglesia de San Miguel. This was built in the 15th century but ravaged by pirates in the late 16th and early 17th centuries, and badly fire-damaged in 1909. Opposite is the town's finest historic house, the Palacio de Spinola, now converted into a museum. Here, you can see how a wealthy 18th-century Genoese merchant family lived. Two other ancient buildings on the square which are open to the public are the Caja de Canarios (Canaries savings bank), which occupies the 15th-century tithe barn, and the Restaurant Acatife, also located in an old mansion.

Adjacent to the main square is the charming Plaza 18 de Julio. The Centro Natural (see pages 142–3), occupies the old hospital building, dating from 1473. In the top left corner of the square (facing the pretty statue of the girl with a pitcher) is the snowy-white Casa Cuartel. This 17th-century balconied house was formerly the local army barracks.

At the top end of town, the handsome 16th-century Convento de San Francisco is also worth a visit. The castle looming over the town is the Castillo de Santa Bárbara (see above). *9km north of Arrecife. Palacio de Spinola museum (tel: 84 51 81). Open: daily, except Wednesday, 9am–2pm. Admission charge.*

The windmill and wine press at the Villa Agrícola el Patio

VILLA AGRÍCOLA EL PATIO

Lanzarote's newest tourist attraction is a small group of old agricultural buildings, beautifully restored to illustrate life on the land between 50 and 100 years ago. An enthusiastic guide (speaking Spanish only) will show you into a windmill, a great barn converted to a museum, a *bodega* (wine store) and outhouses with various types of hand-powered mills and, to end the tour, you will be given a taste of local wine, cheese and breadsticks in an atmospheric bar area.

Tiagua (Sóo road), 12km northwest of Arrecife. No telephone. Open: Monday to Friday, 10am–5pm; Saturday, 10am–2pm. Admission charge.

Fields of Fire

This extraordinary walk through the Parque
Nacional de Timanfaya is the perfect complement
to the spectacular Route of the Volcanoes coach
tour (see page 69) and should answer everything
you want to know about this alien landscape.
Because the walk is within the highly sensitive
protected area of the National Park it may only be
undertaken with a guide from ICONA, the Spanish Nature
Conservancy body (see pages 137–8) and must be booked
in advance (tel: 84 02 38/40). There is no charge for this
tour and anyone who is reasonably active may join it.
*Allow total time, including 30 minutes' vehicle
transportation, of around 3 hours.*

Start at the Camel Park Geology Museum.

CAMEL PARK GEOLOGY MUSEUM

This small museum provides an introduction to the cataclysmic
events of 1730–6 which shaped the terrain you are about to cross.
*From here you will be transported to the start of the walk, just north
of Yaiza, by ICONA minibus.*

TREMESANA

The walk starts alongside the volcano of Tremesana. This
predates the 18th-century eruptions and vegetation has started
to reclaim its slopes. Tremesana is just below Montaña Rajada,

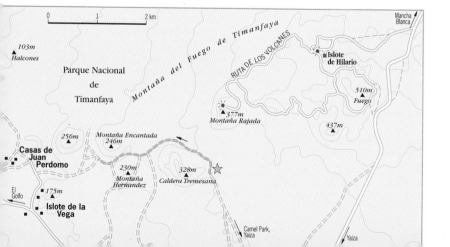

on top of which is the spectacular *mirador* visited on the park's own *Ruta de Los Volcanes* coach tour. Note the fig trees growing in the stone half-circles which protect the crops from wind. Even here, near the epicentre of the destruction, it is possible to grow crops. One particular stone half-circle is unique: look for it on the side of Tremesana, cleverly buttressed to stop it sliding down the mountain. Your guide will also show you a fig-drying circle. *The walk continues alongside the fissure.*

FISSURE LINE

From the *mirador* you will have had an eagle's eye view of this great rent in the earth which runs from Montaña Rajada to Montaña Encantada, caused by the exploding magma. En route you will learn about different types of lava and the flora and fauna that eke an existence in the National Park. You may see a locust blown over from Africa, a rabbit, a hawk or raven, or perhaps even the park's nesting vultures.

THE LAVA LAKE

Lava, gushing forth from the great tear in the earth at up to 70kph, formed a lake (long-since dry) some 5m deep at this point. Peer down into the fissures which reach to the bottom.

VOLCANIC TUBES

Volcanic gases and lava running underground have formed countless tunnels just below the surface of Lanzarote. Your guide will point out where these occur (from tell-tale signs such as yellow sulphur stains) and if he is sure that it is safe to do so, may invite the group to jump up and down on the spot to hear the hollow sound from beneath. The most famous volcanic

The view from Montaña Rajada of the path of devastation taken by the lava when the volcano erupted. The first explosion occurred on the evening of 1 September 1730 and lasted 19 days. Volcanic activity continued for 6 more years

chambers have been converted into living and exhibition spaces at the Fundación César Manrique (see pages 64–5) but here you can visit two caves in their natural state. One of these was used in the filming of *One Million Years BC* and your guide will take great delight in showing you Raquel Welch's cave!
The walk continues for another 10 minutes, past a quarry, to where the ICONA minibus will collect and return you to the Camel Park.

TENERIFE

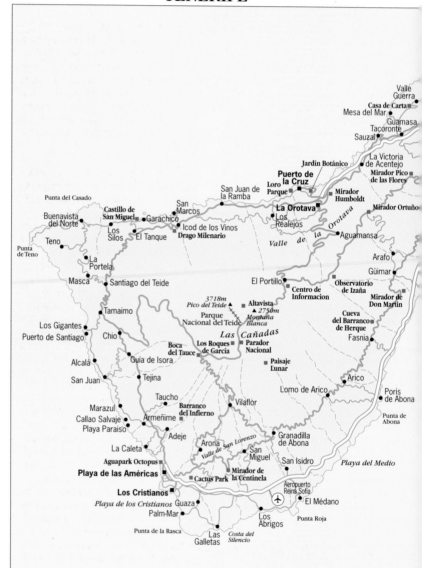

Tenerife

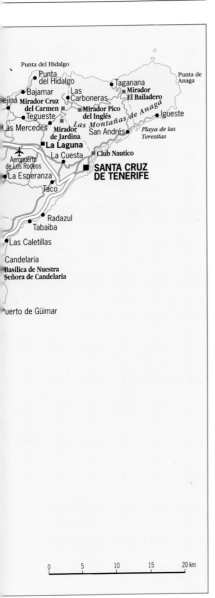

Tenerife is the largest Canary Island and in Mount Teide boasts the highest point in all Spanish territory. Consequently the weather contrasts here are greater than on any other island. In winter the wind may whistle and snow may drift around Mount Teide, while just 40km to the south sunbathers bronze themselves on the beach.

The south of the island is hot, dry and arid, with little of sightseeing interest. Its resorts are the brash new face of Tenerife. For history, culture and scenery you have to go to the north to the fine old colonial towns of La Laguna, La Orotava and the capital, Santa Cruz. Even Puerto de la Cruz, where tourism on Tenerife was born around a century ago, still retains much of its old character, despite its increasing number of high-rise hotels.

The north is green and lush, which, of course, means rain. It's short, sharp and only occasional in summer, but in winter it's almost guaranteed to shave a few days off a two-week stay.

Teide rises above everything on Tenerife. The volcanic scenery of its National Park is out of this world, but there are plenty of other competing attractions on the island. Zoos, gardens, banana plantations and museums mean no-one need ever be at a loose end here.

Surprisingly, the only thing that Tenerife is short on is good beaches. Only the golden strip of Playa de las Teresitas (near Santa Cruz) is worth a postcard home. However, with alternatives such as the Lido at Puerto de la Cruz and Aguapark Octopus at Playa de las Américas, few people seem to mind.

The Anaga Mountains

Despite its great beauty, the panoramic, green-cloaked Anaga Mountains region is still relatively unexplored and small villages, cut off from the main roads, form a genuinely 'hidden Tenerife'. It's an excellent area for walking, and this is the only way to do it justice. However it's also an easy area to tour by car with several fine *miradores* guaranteeing a memorable trip.

BAJAMAR

Bajamar is one of the oldest tourist resorts on the island, popular with German visitors. Like its fellow veteran, Puerto de la Cruz, it has only a small, black beach to offer its guests and so uses pools by the promenade. Unlike Puerto, however, Bajamar has not moved with the times and has a rather tired, dated look about it.

Punta del Hidalgo, 3km to the north, is its newer sister resort, many of its hotels enjoying excellent cliff-top positions. The sunset views from here are said to be the best on Tenerife.

Bajamar is 30km northeast of Puerto de la Cruz.

BOSQUE DE LAS MERCEDES

This is a primeval laurel forest, of the type that can be found on La Gomera (see pages 108–9). This sort of vegetation is now quite rare and much prized by botanists and ecologists. It stretches from north of the village of Las Mercedes to the higher ground of the mountains.

Las Mercedes is 4km north of La Laguna.

CASA DE CARTA

The beautiful 18th-century Canarian house of the Carta family houses the islands' finest ethnographic collection. The house itself is a superlative example of Canarian architecture with an outstanding collection of porticos, patios and richly carved wood-work. Its most colourful exhibits are traditional Canarian costumes, which range from the 18th century to the present day. You can see how these were made in the weaving and needlework rooms.

Other displays include reconstructions of various rooms, a ceramics collection and cereal and *gofio-* (maize meal) related exhibits.

Tacoronte–Valle de Guerra Road, 25km northeast of Puerto de la Cruz (tel: 54 30 53). Open: daily, except Friday, 10am–1pm and 4pm–7pm (summer); 10am–1pm and 3pm–6pm (winter). Admission charge.

MIRADORES (LOOKOUT POINTS)

Cruz del Carmen

Fine views to the mountains (north) and to La Laguna and Teide (south) can be enjoyed from this elevation of 920m. An early 17th-century chapel here holds the much-venerated figure of Nuestra Señora de las Mercedes.

8km northeast of La Laguna.

De Jardina

This is the closest *mirador* to La Laguna and has a splendid view into the fertile 'garden' area which makes up the city hinterland and beyond to the east coast.

7km northeast of La Laguna.

El Bailadero

A spectacular viewpoint perched on a

The Anaga foothills, seen from the Mirador de Jardina (looking south)

knife-edge of rock, giving 360° views. The town straggling down to the north coast directly below is Taganana. *19km northeast of La Laguna.*

Pico del Inglés

One explanation for this curious name ('Peak of the English') is that, in the days of Raleigh and Hawkins, English spies sent signals from here to their marauding ships down below whenever a Spanish galleon was sighted. It is the loftiest (992m) and the best of all the Anaga vantage points, with a striking panorama of the mountains and (on a clear day) views as far south as Gran Canaria. *9km northeast of La Laguna.*

TAGANANA

This pretty, white village is strung out along the hillside which plunges steeply towards the coast. There are beaches just 2km further north, but these are not suitable for swimming due to their dangerous undertow. *24km northeast of La Laguna.*

La Laguna

*L*a Laguna (officially San Cristóbal de la Laguna) was founded in 1496 by the island conqueror, Alonso Fernández de Lugo as capital of all the Canaries. It remained the main city until the early 18th century and its numerous handsome 16th- and 17th-century mansions attest to the wealth of this era. Despite its wonderful architecture and Spanish atmosphere, it is almost untouched by tourism. Today it is the most important town on the island after Santa Cruz, and its university gives it a youthful air in spite of its antiquity.

Sightseeing here is easy. Start in the unmissable main square of Plaza del Adelantado at the *ayuntamiento* (town hall), where you should be able to pick up a town map. Walk up Calle Obispo Rey Redondo, then return via the parallel street of Calle San Agustín.

CALLE OBISPO REY REDONDO

This ancient street possesses many fine buildings. Aside from the Casa de los Capitanes, the Cathedral, and the Iglesia de la Nuestra Señora de la Concepción (see below), look out for the Teatro Leal, an overbearing pink and yellow confection with two bright red cupolas, dating from 1915. Near the top of the street is the charming Plaza de la Concepción, where lovely old houses

look onto a square with two dragon trees and a bizarre Art Nouveau structure covers an electricity sub-station.

CALLE SAN AGUSTÍN

Walking towards the Plaza del Adelantado, look out for the following highlights on this most handsome of streets : Instituto Cabrera Pinto, a fine 16th-century ex-convent building with a graceful bell tower; Palacio Episcopal (Bishop's Palace), a 17th-century palace with a beautiful patio open to the public (*daily 9am–1pm and 4–6pm*); Museu de Historia (see below); Consejo Consultivo de Canarias, no 16 – peep inside to see the perfect patio of this 1746 house.

CASA DE LOS CAPITANES
(House of the Captains)

This splendid former residence of the island's Captain Generals dates back some 250 years. It is now part of the town hall and is open to the public during office hours. Go upstairs to see its splendid wooden panelling and its Moorish wooden-trellised oriel window. *Calle Obispo Rey Redondo (tel: 26 10 11). Open: 9am–1pm and 4pm–7pm. Admission free.*

La Laguna's Historical Museum is the finest in the Canaries

CATEDRAL (Cathedral)

A cavernous, awe-inspiring church, founded in 1515 but remodelled in 1904–5. There are many treasures to admire and behind the High Altar is the simple tomb of de Lugo.

Plaza Fray Albino, off Calle Obispo Rey Redondo (tel: 25 89 39). Open: Monday to Saturday, 8am–1.30pm and 5pm–7.30pm.

IGLESIA DE NUESTRA SEÑORA DE LA CONCEPCIÓN (Church of Our Lady of the Conception)

This splendid church is the oldest in La Laguna, built in 1502. It has changed little over the centuries and its woodwork, particularly the ceiling, shows outstanding craftsmanship.

Calle Obispo Rey Redondo (tel: 26 19 13). Open: Monday to Friday, 10am–noon.

The imposing cathedral of Santa Iglesia

MUSEU DE HISTORIA DE TENERIFE

This recently opened museum charts the history of the island from the Conquest to the present day with a series of very well displayed exhibits. The star attraction is the building itself, the Casa de Lercaro, built in 1593.

Lercaro House, Calle San Agustin, 22 (tel: 63 01 21). Open: Tuesday to Saturday, 10am–5pm; Sunday, 10am–2pm. Admission charge.

PLAZA DEL ADELANTADO

This is probably the best architectural ensemble in the archipelago. Start at the neo-classical 19th-century *ayuntamiento* (top left-hand corner). To the right is the Convent of Santa Catalina, with an unusual lattice-work gallery. Adjacent is the Palacio de Nava, a colonial baroque palace. On the opposite side of the

square, the Mercado Municipal also has a latticed gallery. Next to it is the charming, tiny Ermita de San Miguel, built in 1507 by order of Lugo. It's now an exhibition hall.

Convent of Santa Catalina. Open: Monday to Saturday, 4pm–6pm; Sunday, 10am–noon and 4–6pm. Admission free.

Ancient houses on Calle San Agustin

La Orotava

*L*a Orotava is a beautifully preserved old colonial town of steep, cobbled streets. Most visitors go only to the showpiece Casas de los Balcones; the rest of town is virtually untouched by tourism. La Orotava is also the craft centre of Tenerife. The finest view of town and the best place to start exploring is in the raised balcony-like Plaza de la Constitución; everything is within 5 to 10 minutes' walk of here.

CASAS DE LOS BALCONES
(Houses of the Balconies)
This is the quintessential colonial Canarian building, named after the superbly crafted balconies which look on to the courtyard within. The tropical patio, full of exotic greenery, an ancient wine press, old pictures and pottery, conjures up an evocative atmosphere of early colonial days.

The houses, joined together, date from the 1630s and, as you can see from an upper-floor museum, were home to a wealthy family. The rest of the building is a craft and souvenirs shop, popular for its

traditionally dressed embroiderers and its 'sand-painting' demonstrations.

The Casa de Turista, opposite, is a house of similar style and age, built in 1590. It, too, is a craft and gift shop. *Calle San Francisco (tel: 38 28 55). Open: Monday to Friday, 9am–1.30pm and 4pm–7.30pm; Saturday, 9am–1.30pm. Admission free.*

CASA TORREHERMOSA
This is the official Empresa Insular de

The symmetrical elegance of a traditional Canarian balcony, La Orotava

Artesanía (island enterprise craft workshop), and it too is based in an ancient colonial house together with a small museum of island crafts.

Next door, in the Convento de Santo Domingo, is the modest Museo de Artesanía Iberoamericana (Museum of Spanish-American crafts).
Calle Tomás Zerolo (tel: 33 40 13). Open: Monday to Saturday, 9.30am–1pm and 3pm–6.30pm. Admission free. Convento: see notice on door for opening times.

HIJUELA DEL BOTÁNICO

The name of this garden, 'Daughter of the Botanic Garden', explains its relationship with its famous 'parent' near by in Puerto de la Cruz (see pages 94–5). It is a small densely planted area claiming over 3,000 different tropical and sub-tropical species.
Calle Hermano Apolinar. Open: daily, dawn to dusk. Admission free.

HOSPITAL DE LA SANTÍSIMA TRINIDAD (Hospital of the Holy Trinity)

Formerly an 18th-century convent, this is now a hospital which cares for mentally handicapped patients. The revolving drum set into the main door was used to donate gifts anonymously.

The view from the terrace of the hospital over the Orotava Valley was once one of the great sights of this region. Today it is still worth seeing, though marred by urban development.
Calle San Francisco (tel: 33 02 00). Open: Monday to Saturday, 4–5.30pm; Sunday, 10.30am–noon. Admission free.

IGLESIA DE NUESTRA SEÑORA DE LA CONCEPCIÓN (Church of Our Lady of the Conception)

Along with its namesake in La Laguna,

Plaza de Franco, the scene of La Orotava's famous Corpus Christi flower carpets celebrations

this is probably the finest church on the island. It's an extravagant, handsome baroque structure with twin onion-topped towers and a large yellow dome, built between 1768 and 1788. Its screen, altar, statuary and carved choir stalls are regarded as masterpieces.
Plaza Casañas (tel. 33 01 87). Open: usually masses only.

Near La Orotava

MUSEO DE CERÁMICA (Pottery Museum)

A collection of around 1,000 pieces of pottery is held in this typical (though much-restored) early 17th-century house. Potters give demonstrations.
La Luz–Las Candias road, 2km west of La Orotava (free bus from Playa Martiánez, Puerto de la Cruz). Tel: 33 33 96. Open: daily, 10am–6pm. Admission charge.

Parque Nacional del Teide

Mount Teide is, at 3,718m, the highlight of Tenerife in every sense, with a dramatic volcanic landscape unrivalled in the Eastern Canary islands. Conditions in the National Park vary dramatically. In winter, snow falls, gale-force winds blow and the roads are sometimes closed off. In summer, even this arid landscape is aglow with plants and flowers and daytime temperatures can soar above 40°C (though the summit of Teide is still chilly). Your journey from the coast may mostly be in the clouds, but just before you arrive at the cable car, these will roll back to reveal bright blue skies and the omnipresent mountain will be revealed.

EL PORTILLO VISITORS INFORMATION CENTRE

The El Portillo office, at the eastern entrance to the National Park, offers a small exhibition and information area. You can join a walking tour here, free of charge, with an ICONA guide (see page 137–8). Telephone ahead to book your place. If you intend walking on your own in the park you should still call in here for maps and advice. Note – walking in the park can be dangerous in winter.
32km south of Puerto de la Cruz. Open: daily, 9am–4pm. Tel (ICONA Santa Cruz office): 29 01 29/29 01 83.

EL TELEFÉRICO (Cable Car)

Unless you are a keen hill climber this is the only way to reach the summit of Teide. The car ascends from an altitude of 2,356m to 3,555m in eight minutes, which still leaves you a 20-minute slog in

The cable car to the summit of Mount Teide

A LITTLE HISTORY

About 3 million years ago, a giant volcano near the present Mount Teide (but much, much bigger) exploded and/or collapsed in on itself. The volcano walls, or what was left of them, formed a *caldera* (crater) in which Teide and other volcanoes now stand. The *caldera* measures 48km in circumference, and some parts of the wall still stand up to 500m high. It may be impossible to visualise this from ground level, but as you gaze upon the torn and twisted earth try to imagine the awesome power that turned the earth into this alien lunarscape.

The dramatic formations of Los Roques, with the gullied slopes of Mount Teide in the background

thin air up the last 163m. At the summit is an iron cross, a sulphurous smell and (on a clear day) views of all the other islands and perhaps North Africa.

Note – the car does not operate when it is too windy (which is frequently the case in winter), and in summer long queues often form.

43km south of Puerto de la Cruz (tel: 38 37 11/28 78 37). The car operates daily (weather permitting), 9am–4pm.

LOS ROQUES DE GARCÍA (The Rocks of García)

Los Roques is probably the most spectacular grouping of pyroclastic debris within the park and certainly the best within easy access of the road. For that reason it is on every coach tour itinerary and the rocks are often swarming with day-trippers. It would be hard to detract from such a magnificent sight as this, however, with views to Teide on one side and, on the other, the great flat expanse of the Llano (plain) de Ucanca. This is one of the park's many *cañadas* – yellow sedimentary plains where fine debris has accumulated.

Across the road from Los Roques is the Parador de Cañadas del Teide.

Close to Los Roques, heading south, is the rock formation known as Los Azulejos (*azulejos* are glazed tiles), where the rocks glint green with iron hydrate deposits.

47km south of Puerto de la Cruz.

FLORA

There are nearly 2,000 different species of plants in the Canary Islands, of which around 700 are endemic (exclusive to the islands). Many are only of interest to botanists, but the species mentioned below are all quite remarkable and can usually be seen without ever having to leave the beaten track.

The biggest and most famous inhabitant of the islands is the dragon tree. A peculiarity of this tree is its lack of rings, which means that telling its age is very difficult. The largest and oldest tree, the Drago Milenario (at Icod de los Vinos, Tenerife), is between 500 and 3,000 years old. Guanches attributed magical properties to the tree and used its 'dragon's blood' sap (which turns red in the air) to heal wounds.

Other strange Canarian trees are the twisted and dead-looking *sabinas* (junipers) of El Hierro, while the protected *laurasilva* laurel forest of La Gomera is a wet, dark, spooky place to explore. By way of contrast, the tall, light, graceful Canary Pine is found on higher ground on all the western islands and Gran Canaria. The endemic tree of the dry eastern islands is the Canary date palm (which does not produce fruit), a close relative of the North African variety. Flora that do bear a harvest are the banana plant and the almond tree, both of which are imports.

The prettiest plants on the islands

Top, far left: the famous 3,000-year-old dragon tree of Icod de los Vinos (Tenerife).
Left: a prickle of cacti.
Below and bottom, far left: orchids and strelitzias in the subtropical Palmitos Parque at Maspalomas (Gran Canaria)

– bougainvillea, hibiscus, poinsettia and the graceful *strelitzia* (bird-of-paradise flower) have also been brought here from other countries.

The largest and most striking endemic flower is the slender red viper's bugloss or *tajinaste* (*echium wildpretii*), which grows up to 2m high in the Cañadas del Teide park. Also here (and in many other places) is the yellow or white *retama*, or Teide broom, which gives off a wonderful, pungent-sweet scent.

The most noticeable plants of the drier regions are the new world cacti, prickly pears, imported to attract cochineal bugs (see pages 72–3) and the endemic cactus-like *cardón* (*euphorbia canariensis*). This is a candelabra spurge with tall smooth stems (like organ pipes in appearance), very common in the south of Gran Canaria. Other succulents include several species of *senecios* and *tabaibas* – small spiky plants, resembling yucca trees, which are very tenacious and soon colonise deserted house roofs.

Northwestern Tenerife

*T*he northwest corner of Tenerife is a highly rewarding area for exploration. The countryside of the Teno Hills is as beautiful as any scenery to the northeast, and Garachico and Icod de los Vinos are two of the island's most charming small towns.

GARACHICO

This modest fishing port hides an outstanding collection of ancient buildings among its narrow cobbled streets. Yet in 1706 it was all but destroyed by lava flowing down to the sea. To appreciate how Garachico was rebuilt on the lava peninsula that formed here, approach it on the C820 from Icod de los Vinos and as you descend the hillside via El Tanque you will enjoy a splendid bird's-eye view.

The most notable survivor of the disaster is the beautifully preserved seafront Castillo de San Miguel (Castle of St Michael), which dates from the 16th century. It now houses a small museum of fossils and shells.

Near by is the port, which until 1706, was the most important in Tenerife

because of its fine natural harbour. On the town side is a charming square with a beautiful sunken garden. A 16th-century arch and a 17th-century wine press adorn this flower-filled space. From here there is a view of the 18th-century Iglesia de Santa Ana (Church of St Anna). The town's most beautiful church is the 16th-century Iglesia de San Francisco (Church of St Francis), in the adjacent square. The old convent next door now houses a cultural centre, Casa de Cultura.

At the other end of town is the 17th-century Convento de Santo Domingo, now home to the Museo de Arte Contemporaneo (Museum of Contemporary Art).

Garachico is 31km west of Puerto de la Cruz (via El Tanque). Castillo de San

Garachico offered the best harbour on Tenerife's north coast until it was engulfed by lava in 1706

Miguel museum (tel: 83 00 00). Open:
Monday to Friday, 9am–7pm; Saturday
and Sunday, 9am–1pm. Admission charge.
Casa de Cultura, Plaza de San Francisco
(tel: 83 00 00). Open: Monday to Friday,
9am–7pm; Saturday and Sunday,
9am–1pm. Museo de Arte Contemporaneo,
Plaza Santo Domingo (tel: 83 00 00).
Open: Monday to Saturday, 10am–1pm
and 3pm–6pm; Sunday, 10am–1pm.
Admission charge.

ICOD DE LOS VINOS
Icod de los Vinos is famous for its
1,000-year-old dragon tree (Drago
Milenario). The real age of this monster
is unknown, but it is the oldest dragon
tree in existence and, at over 16m tall
and with a girth of 6m, it is also the
largest. The classic view of the tree is
from the Plaza de la Iglesia, which
boasts fine exotic greenery of its own
and hosts the beautiful 15th- to 16th-
century Iglesia de San Marcos (Church
of St Mark). However, there is an even
more scenic view from below, which
includes a very tall palm tree and an
archetypal Canarian balcony.
20km west of Puerto de la Cruz.

LOS GIGANTES/PUERTO DE
SANTIAGO
A quiet, low-rise, up-market holiday
development has sprung up here to take
advantage of the dramatic sea-cliff
setting of Los Gigantes and the black
sandy beach next to Puerto de Santiago.
Massive cliffs drop almost sheer into the
sea from a height of 500m.
42km north of Playa de las Américas.

MASCA
The tip of the northwest is covered by
the Teno Hills – one of the most
picturesque corners of the island, rent

Masca's dramatic site attracts many visitors

by deep ravines and cloaked in lush
greenery. The road south from
Buenavista del Norte passes along steep,
narrow hairpin-bends and leads to the
village of Masca. Until recently it was
virtually 'undiscovered', but now Masca
is on most coach excursion itineraries.
Despite the occasional crowds, however,
its magical site cannot be diminished. Its
houses are set on narrow ridges which
plunge down into a verdant valley of
dramatic rock formations.
20km southwest of Garachico via
Buenavista del Norte.

Puerto de Santiago and the Los Gigantes seacliffs

Puerto de la Cruz

Puerto de la Cruz, or Puerto, as it is known, is the longest established and most complete holiday resort on Tenerife. It has a magnificent backdrop, with Teide towering above and the lush Orotava Valley sweeping down to the city.

Unlike most Canarian resorts this is a town with its own identity, where locals still live, work, eat and drink. The British put Puerto on the map as a holiday destination around a century ago, but today's town is still very much abreast of the times. In addition to its old-world charms it features some high quality visitor attractions on its outskirts.
Puerto de la Cruz is 60km northwest of Reina Sofía airport. Tourist office: Plaza de la Iglesia, 3 (tel: 38 60 00). Open: daily, 9am–7pm.

BANANERA EL GUANCHE

Despite its obvious mass tourist appeal the cultivation of this miniature banana plantation is well explained and its lush, terraced gardens hold an extensive range of indigenous and exotic plants. There is an area of over 400 cacti and a small collection of farmyard animals.
3km southeast of Puerto on La Orotava road (tel: 33 18 53). Open: daily,

9am–6pm. Admission charge. Free bus from Playa Martiánez.

JARDÍN BOTÁNICO (Botanic Garden)

This is the oldest of Puerto's attractions, founded in 1788 by King Carlos III as a halfway-house Jardín de Aclimatación (Acclimatisation Garden) for plants travelling from the tropics to Spain. It's a small, shady place with over 200 species of plants and trees crowding into just 2.5 hectares. Most people's favourite is the giant 200-year-old South American fig tree in the centre, a menacing gothic mass of intertwined roots and branches.

If you prefer flowers to trees and shrubs, La Rosaleda rose gardens are near by with over 15,000 roses and waterplants, plus free-roaming peacocks, cranes, pheasants and ducks.
Jardín Botánico 2km southeast of centre, Calle Retama on La Orotava road (tel: 38 52 72). Open: daily, 9am–6pm. Admission charge. La Rosaleda 3km southeast of centre, Calle Camino Lazo. Open: daily, 9am–6pm. Admission charge. Free bus from Playa Martiánez.

LIDO/LAGO MARTIÁNEZ (Lido/Pool Martiánez)

Until the opening of Puerto's Playa Jardín (see below) the Lido Martiánez was the town's unofficial 'beach'. It was designed by César Manrique (see pages

The exotic terraced gardens of Bananera el Guanche

Marine flippery at the new dolphinarium, Loro Parque

66–7) in 1969 and brilliantly solved the problem of Puerto's beachless seafront. This beautifully laid out series of pools and fountains, palm-shaded sunbathing terraces and black and white lava rockery covers 3 hectares and attracts over one million visitors per year.
Playa Martiánez (tel: 38 38 52). Open: daily, 9am–6pm. Admission charge.

LORO PARQUE (PARROT PARK)

This Florida-style wildlife park is the most popular paying-visitor attraction on the islands and maintains very high standards of both conservation and entertainment. Set in superb tropical gardens, it was conceived as a parrot park and is said to contain the world's largest collection of parrots. It has also recently added the largest dolphinarium outside America, a huge aquarium which claims the largest underwater tunnel in the world, a gorilla jungle and a bat cave. Other attractions include a 180° special effects cinema, parrot shows, performing sealions, flamingos, crocodiles, chimpanzees and tigers.
Calle San Felipe (free buses from Playa Martiánez and Playa de las Américas), 3km west in Punta Brava district (tel: 38 30 12). Open: daily, 8.30am–5pm. Admission charge.

PLAYA JARDÍN

This new black-sand beach was opened in 1992–3. The crashing Atlantic waves have been tamed by a man-made reef comprising some 4,000 20-tonne concrete blocks (submerged out of sight) and the back of the beach area was landscaped under the direction of César Manrique (see pages 66–7). Adjacent is the 17th-century Castillo de San Felipe, which is to be re-opened as a cultural centre.

The lido de Martiánez, 3.2 hectares of recreational abandonment

Santa Cruz

Santa Cruz is the capital of Tenerife and the administrative centre of the western islands. It's also an important port. To most holiday visitors, however, it means a morning's 'tax-free' shopping in the Calle del Castillo and a visit to the town's most colourful bazaar, the Mercado de Nuestra Señora de África.

Santa Cruz is more than just a place to shop; it's a busy, though rarely stressful, typical Canarian town with a grand, somewhat faded air.
Santa Cruz is 36km northeast of Puerto de la Cruz. Tourist office: Cabildo Insular, Plaza de España (tel: 60 55 92). Open: Monday to Saturday, 8am–5.45pm.

IGLESIA DE NUESTRA SEÑORA DE LA CONCEPCIÓN (Church of Our Lady of the Conception)
This early 16th-century church is the most important historical building in Santa Cruz. Unfortunately, it is currently closed for restoration. Enquire at the tourist office. *Plaza de la Iglesia.*

SANTA CRUZ DE TENERIFE

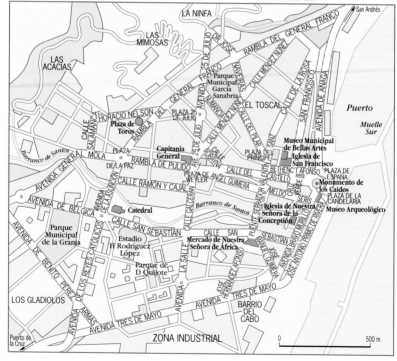

MERCADO DE NUESTRA SEÑORA DE ÁFRICA (Market of Our Lady of Africa)

This bustling market is colourful and vibrant, selling a wide range of fruits, vegetables, flowers, fish and meats. On Sundays a *rastro* (flea-market) is held next to the halls.

Across Puerte Serrador. Open: Monday to Saturday, 9am–1pm.

MUSEO MUNICIPAL DE BELLAS ARTES (Municipal Museum of Fine Arts)

The pride of this museum is its fine collection of works by Flemish and Spanish masters, including Ribera, Brueghel, Van Loo and Jordaens.

Calle José Murphy (tel: 24 43 58). Open: Monday to Saturday, 1pm–8pm (winter), 10am–8pm (summer). Admission charge.

PARQUE MUNICIPAL GARCÍA SANABRIA

This beautifully laid out mature park is a fine place to stroll. Exotic trees and shrubs, fountains and statuary, a floral clock and a small animal compound are its main attractions.

En route to the park are two delightful plazas. Plaza del General Weyler is a popular, flower-filled meeting point. Plaza 25 de Julio is a tiny, round space with unusual ceramic benches, colourfully decorated with museum-piece 1920s tiles, carrying advertising messages.

Rambla del General Franco–Mendez Nuñez.

PLAZA DE ESPAÑA

The drab, towering cross which stands in this square and marks the hub of Santa Cruz is a monument to the dead of the Spanish Civil War (1936–9). Next to it is another depressing example of Fascist Architecture, the huge, grey *Cabildo*

The government offices in Plaza de España

Insular (island government offices). At the side of the building is the entrance to the Museo Arqueológico (Archaeological Museum), which deals with pre-Conquest history (see pages 10–11). There are a few interesting Guanche exhibits illustrating curious early medical practices and belief in the after life (mummies); information is only in Spanish.

Tel: 60 55 74: Open: Monday to Friday, 9am–1pm and 4–6pm; Saturday, 9am–1pm. Admission charge.

PLAZA DE LA CANDELARIA

The centre of this square is dominated by a statue illustrating El Triunfo de la Candelaria (Triumph of the Virgin of Candelaria – see pages 98–9) by the renowned Italian sculptor Antonio Canova (1757–1822). The figures on guard at the corner represent Guanche chieftains (see pages 10–11).

Look into the bank at No 9 on the Plaza. This was formerly the Palacio de Carta, built in 1742, and contains a perfect example of a Canarian patio.

Calle del Castillo, leading off from here, is the town's main shopping street.

Southern Resorts

*T*he once separate resorts of Los Cristianos and Playa de las Américas have now all but joined to become the second largest resort in the Canary Islands (after Maspalomas on Gran Canaria) and one of the biggest in all Spain. The reason for their success is based on two factors: all-year-round sunshine and an ability to cater for hundreds of thousands of package holidaymakers a year.

BARRANCO DEL INFIERNO

Despite its fearsome name ('Hell's Gorge') this lush ravine is the only place where you will find natural running water in the harsh and arid landscape of southern Tenerife. It is a popular beauty spot for walking. The walk along the ravine is signposted and takes around 2½ hours there and back.
6km north of Playa de las Américas.

EL ABRIGO

There are few places in the south where good local restaurants may easily be found, and picturesque fishing villages are even scarcer. So it is no surprise that El Abrigo is such a popular (and expensive) place to sample the local fish.
15km east of Los Cristianos.

The busy port of Los Cristianos

EL MÉDANO

This small, developing resort has the best of the southern beaches but with gusts that often sandblast its occupants.
22km east of Los Cristianos.

LOS CRISTIANOS

Until quite recently Los Cristianos was a humble port for shipping tomatoes. Since the 1970s, however, it has become one of the most popular resorts in the Canary Islands. It draws a slightly older clientèle than Playa de las Américas and has two advantages over its neighbour. Firstly, if you look hard among the new developments you can still find vestiges of the old settlement. Secondly, its harbour provides a changing mix of fishing boats, pleasure craft and ferries chugging to and from La Gomera.

There is a sandy beach which looks on to the harbour, but it is much too small for the great demand put upon it.

Near by are Cactus and Animal Park, a large cactus garden with a collection of small animals and birds; Jardines del Atlantico Bananera, a guided tour around a banana plantation; Amazonia, a large tropical garden with free-flying butterflies and humming birds; Tenerife Zoo and Monkey Park.
All open daily 10am–6pm (free bus from

Dining al fresco on Playa de las Américas

Los Cristianos or Playa de las Américas). Los Cristianos is 15km west of Reina Sofía airport. Cactus and Animal Park is on the Las Galletas road, between Los Cristianos and Guaza (tel: 79 54 24). Jardines del Atlantico Bananera, Buzanada, between Las Galletas and Valle de San Lorenzo (tel: 72 04 03). Amazonia is near exit 26 Autopista Sur (tel: 79 54 24). Tenerife Zoo and Monkey Park, Llano Azul (tel: 75 13 68).

PLAYA DE LAS AMÉRICAS

A boom-town resort of considerable proportions, Playa de las Américas was built from scratch in the late 1960s as a home-from-home for north European package holidaymakers. There is little that is Canarian and unless you are happy drinking pints of British beer and eating food 'just like Mother makes', then this place probably isn't for you.

Beaches are dark sand but well laid, but sheer numbers mean that there is hardly room to shake a towel. Many tourists simply decamp to Aguapark (waterpark) Octopus, at San Eugenio.
17km west of Reina Sofía airport. Tourist office: front of Parque Santiago II. Tel: 79 76 68. Open: Monday to Friday 9am–3.30pm. Aguapark Octopus, San Eugenio, 2km east of the centre (tel: 79 22 66). Open: 10am daily. Admission charge.

THE EAST COAST

The major point of interest on Tenerife's east coast is the Basilica of Candelaria (17km south of Santa Cruz). This holds a statue of the patron saint of all the Canary Islands, Nuestra Señora de la Candelaria. The statues on the Plaza de la Candelaria represent Guanche chieftains, who once worshipped the same Virgin.

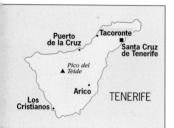

Anaga Peninsula Drive

This excursion takes in the highlights of the north-east peninsula, from the green peaks of the Anaga mountains to the golden sands of Playa de las Teresitas. Choose a clear day to get the best from the *miradores* (viewpoints) en route. (This drive may also be combined with the walk on pages 104–5.) *Aim to arrive at the Casa de Carta museum as it opens at 10am (closed Friday), then allow around 3 hours, excluding stops, to reach Las Teresitas beach.*

Start from Tacoronte.

1 TACORONTE

This straggling town 20km east of Puerto de la Cruz, is famous for its wine and two fine churches; the 17th-century Iglesia de Santa Catalina and close by the Iglesia del Cristo de los Dolores, which holds a much revered 17th-century statue of Christ.
Take the TF122 north, noting the ancient dragon tree as you are leaving town.

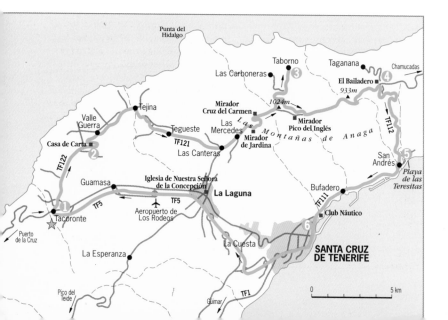

2 CASA DE CARTA (nr Valle Guerra)

An excellent ethnographic museum in an 18th-century house (see page 82). Open 10am–1pm and 4–7pm summer (3–6pm winter); closed Friday.

Continue on the TF122 for 4km, turn right at Tejina onto the TF121 and continue for 12km through Tegueste, Las Canteras and Las Mercedes, stopping to admire the miradores de Jardina and Cruz del Carmen (see pages 82–3). After another 1½km turn left (signposted towards Las Carboneras). Continue straight ahead, ignoring the second Carboneras sign, to Taborno (13km past Cruz del Carmen).

3 TABORNO

This small village is situated high among the Anaga peaks at 1,024m and consequently enjoys marvellous views.
Retrace your route to where you turned left towards Las Carboneras. Carry straight on, then rejoin the main TF1123 road. This scenic road continues for 8km along the top of the cumbre (ridge), with views to north and south, offering a glimpse of the golden sands of Las Teresitas. Turn off left towards El Bailadero.

4 EL BAILADERO

A spectacular *mirador* (see page 83), at which point you can either turn round and go south (left) to Las Teresitas beach and Santa Cruz, go south and then turn north to Taganana (see pages 82), or continue east (straight ahead) for 6km to Chamucadas, where there is another fine *mirador*. Shortly after which the road ends.
From El Bailadero head south on the TF112 to San Andrés.

5 PLAYA DE LAS TERESITAS

It is estimated that this golden strip,

The spectacular and lush Anaga Mountains around Taborno

brought over from the Sahara, constitutes some 4 million sackfuls of sand. It is a superb beach with safe shallow waters and mountain backdrops; well maintained, it is rarely very busy and is unspoilt by surrounding developments. The adjacent village of San Andrés is renowned for its fish restaurants. Notice its ruined castle, neatly smashed in half by a flood tide some 30 years ago.
Continue back along the coastal road for 8km to the waterfront of Santa Cruz.

6 SANTA CRUZ

Just before you reach the centre of town, look for the Club Náutico (Yacht Club), beside which are the remains of the Castillo de Paso Alto. From here Santa Cruz enjoyed its finest military moment in 1797, repulsing an attack by Admiral Lord Nelson and shooting off the lower part of his right arm to boot.

It's often surprisingly easy to park close to the centre of town on the main road – early evening, as the streets come alive again, is a good time to visit the capital.

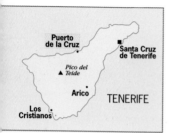

Puerto de la Cruz Walk

Puerto de la Cruz remains at heart a Spanish colonial town with many tangible reminders of its past. This walk will show you a little of the town's history and architecture. Avoid Monday if you wish to visit the Archaeological Museum. *Allow 1–1½ hours (excluding time spent in the Museum).*

Start from the El Peñon (the rock) religious monument, next to the football stadium.

1 CALLE DE SAN FELIPE

This is a charming old street of one-storey fishermen's houses and some good local restaurants. Look out for the unusual green decorated oriel window at no 16.
Turn left into Calle de Pérez Zamora, and left again into Calle de Lomo.

2 CALLE DE LOMO

The Museo Arqueológico (Archaeological Museum) is housed in a fine 19th-century mansion. It stages temporary exhibitions.
Retrace your steps to Calle de San Felipe.

3 PLAZA DEL CHARCO

This handsome square marks the centre of town. Look into the

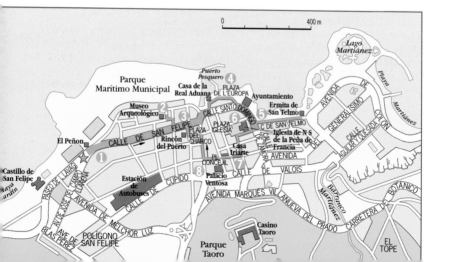

Rincón del Puerto, a fine typical Canarian balconied courtyard, built in 1739.
Continue on Calle de San Felipe and turn left.

4 PUERTO PESQUERO (FISHING PORT)

To the right-hand side of the port the beautiful black and white stone house is the Casa de la Real Aduana (Royal Custom House), the oldest building in town, dating from 1620. Note the fortifications to the seaward side. On the opposite side of the street is the Casa Miranda, dating from around 1730.

A little further on is a new square with cannons, the Plaza de l'Europe, from where there are good sea views. To the right are the Casas Consistoriales (town hall offices, built 1973).
Turn left onto Calle de San Telmo.

5 CALLE DE SAN TELMO

The start of this promenade is known as the Punta del Viento (Windy Point), marked by a modern sculpture of a windswept girl. Below, the waves break spectacularly into the black-lava rockpools. The tiny, snow-white Ermita de San Telmo (Church of St Elmo) dates from the 18th century.

Just strolling on Calle de San Telmo

Retrace your steps to the start of the promenade, continue on for a few yards then turn right into Calle La Hoya, which leads to Plaza Iglesia.

6 PLAZA IGLESIA

Note the old-fashioned *bodega* (wine-shop) on the left before entering the square. This is Puerto's loveliest plaza, with an elegant swan fountain in the centre, dating from 1900. The Iglesia de Nuestra Señora de la Peña de Francia (Church of Our Lady of the Rock of France) is a beautiful 16th-century building (its tower was added in 1898) with excellent baroque altarpieces and side-chapels. The Hotel Marquesa (built 1712) and the Hotel Monopol (built 1742), also on the square, both possess typical balconied patios.
Leave the Plaza by Calle Cólogan and take the second street right, Calle Iriarte.

7 CASA IRIARTE

An 18th-century house with a balcony onto the street and a lovely interior patio. It houses craft-sellers (mostly embroidery) and a small naval museum.

8 PALACIO VENTOSA

On the pretty square diagonally opposite the Casa Iriarte is the Colegio San Agustín. This occupies the 18th-century Palacio Ventosa, of which the most notable feature is the tall tower.
Turn right into Calle Blanco. This leads back to the Plaza del Charco.

Museo Arqueológico (tel: 37 14 65). Open: Tuesday to Saturday, 10am–1pm and 5pm–9pm; Sunday, 10am–1pm. Admission charge.
Casa Iriarte (tel: 38 33 11). Shop and museum open: Monday to Saturday, 9.30am–7pm. Admission charge to museum.
Palacio Ventosa. Although not officially open to the public it can be seen at close quarters from the college grounds during term time.

Chinamada Walk

This walk takes you into the heart of the Anaga Mountains, to a village which, until 1993, was cut off from all roads and where the inhabitants still live in caves carved into the mountainside. It's an easy walk to follow and suitable for all ages (much of the first half could be undertaken in a 4-wheel drive vehicle or even an ordinary car, though the track is quite bumpy). *Allow 1½–2 hours.*

Start from Las Carboneras.

1 LAS CARBONERAS
This small village (see pages 100–1 for how to get here)

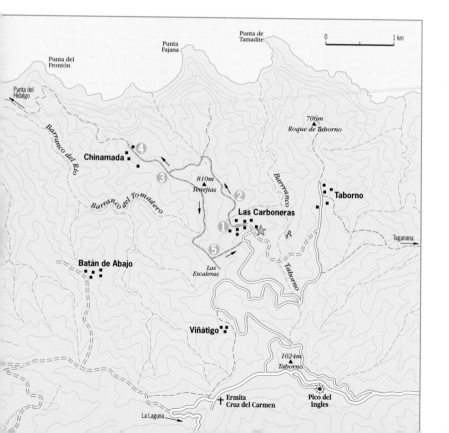

comprises two bars, a church and a handful of houses.

Start by the main plaza and follow the wooden sign, posted to Chinamada (where the road proper finishes and the new track begins).

2 ROQUE DE TABORNO

The first stretch of the walk is dominated by the green, velvety peak of Roque de Taborno, away to your right. This rises to 706m and has a distinctive, bullet-like basalt peak. In winter the wonderful sweet smell of the *retama* plant fills the air along the route.

After around 15 minutes the track turns around the corner away from Roque de Taborno, but still offers fine views. Burrowed into the hillside, caves begin to appear. Turn the next bend and the first cave houses of Chinamada are to the right-hand side of the track. Ignore these and follow the track, which wiggles to the left through a tiny pass and continues ahead.

3 BARRANCO DEL TOMADERO

The view to the left of the track, across the deep green ravine that separates Chinamada from the tiny white houses of Batán, is stunning. This ravine runs all the way to the sea at Punta del Hidalgo. Listen and you will probably hear bells. Goats graze on these seemingly impossibly steep terraced slopes, providing meat and cheese for the people of Chinamada.

4 CHINAMADA

Note the fine dragon tree to the right of the path. A brand new chapel has been built straight ahead of you. The houses of the 30 or so people who live here are small and cut back into the rocky ridge but, as you will see, they are hardly Stone Age. You can walk along the

narrow path alongside the houses. If you are feeling inspired by the scenery, it's around an hour's walk all the way down to Punta del Hidalgo (from where buses run back to La Laguna).

Return the short distance to the small crossroads and climb the hill up the steps to the right, signposted Las Escaleras ('the stairs').

5 LAS ESCALERAS

The steps don't last for long, descending down to a narrow path. This is a pretty route, strewn with ferns and Canary bell flowers. The path initially skirts the hillside; to the right are more fine views across the *barranco*. There's only one route to follow and a metal conduit runs along the side of the path as a guide.

After about 30 minutes you will see the main road down to your left. At this point you can descend and walk back to the village (half a kilometre) or continue along the path for another 10–15 minutes to the Mirador de las Escaleras, which offers yet another fine aspect of these majestic hills. Follow the path back and make the descent to the road.

The path running past Chinamada leads right down to the sea

La Gomera

*L*a Gomera is a dome-shaped island with a sunken central plateau, its sides rent by great gullies which almost completely segment it. This tortuous terrain once presented great communication problems and still adds to journey times. The island may be only 23 by 25km at its widest points, but you won't be able to drive round it comfortably in a day, and a minimum of two days is required to see all the island's highlights.

It would be a shame not to stay overnight on Gomera, since here are arguably the two best hotels in all the Canaries. This really is a case of quality against quantity as, aside from these two, there are no other hotels on the island worthy of the name. The lack of tourism here is at least half of the appeal to the island's small group of admirers. The comparison between La Gomera and Los

LA GOMERA

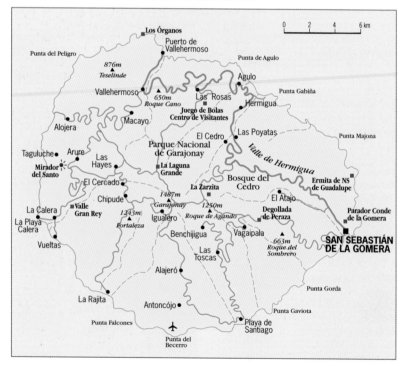

Cristianos, just 32km and 35 minutes away by hydrofoil, is of two wholly different cultures. The gap between them, however, may be about to close a little. For Gomera, so long the only Canary Island without an airport, is about to join the aviation age – albeit only on an inter-island basis. But with only one real beach on the whole island and a limited tourism infrastructure it seems unlikely that La Gomera will go the way of Benidorm.

First impressions here are misleading. The barren landscape around San Sebastián soon gives way to some of the most beautiful, luxuriant valleys in the archipelago, while the centre of the island is almost permanently covered in mist, refreshing the thirsty prehistoric National Park rainforest.

There are few sights as such on Gomera, but natural beauty is here in abundance. To get the best from the island, bring your walking boots and stay for a week.

Above: leading the goats to pastures new
Below: Agulo with Mount Teide in the distance

Northern La Gomera

*T*he road to the north of La Gomera is a spectacular winding route calling at the island's most picturesque settlements. If you have just one day on the island, this is the way to go. It also has the advantage of being lower than the southern route, avoiding the clouds which form on the higher ground. Without these, however, there would be no primordial *laurasilva* forest on Gomera – a feature much enjoyed by walkers and naturalists.

AGULO

The adjectives 'neat and tidy' perfectly describe this small, pretty village of narrow cobbled streets. Its position is perfect – enclosed in a natural amphitheatre of rocky cliffs, perched high above the sea, with Tenerife's Mount Teide forming a majestic backdrop. In the centre is a curiously designed grey and white painted church with Moorish-influenced domes.
25km northwest of San Sebastián.

HERMIGUA

Hermigua, the second largest settlement on the island after San Sebastián, is a long, straggling village clinging to the roadside above a lush valley of banana plantations. Vines are also grown here, strung on bamboo frames which hang diagonally across the hillsides like giant spiders' webs.

Visit the Los Telares craft centre (on the main road) to see the old house where girls still weave on ancient looms. A little further along, stop by the Convento sign. By the side of the plaza is the 16th-century Convento de Santo Domingo, with a fine ceiling and an image of the local saint.
20km northwest of San Sebastián.

JUEGO DE BOLAS CENTRO DE VISITANTES

This excellent visitor centre should be able to answer most questions you may have about La Gomera. Well-labelled gardens illustrate island flora, a small ethnographical museum covers peasant life and a complex of workshops

The children's playground at Vallehermoso – ancient deities or modern art?

demonstrates basketry, weaving, pottery and woodworking. In the main reception area are displays giving information about the Garajonay National Park (see below).

The road between the Visitor Centre and the El Tabor bar leads to a newly created *mirador* with spectacular views right down on top of Agulo (see above) and across to Tenerife. The unsurfaced track at the end of the asphalt road may be very bumpy, but is quite short and manageable in an ordinary car.

The visitor centre is 34km northwest of San Sebastián (tel: 80 09 93). Open: Tuesday to Saturday, 9am–4.30pm.

PARQUE NACIONAL DE GARAJONAY (Garajonay National Park)

This 4,000-hectare National Park occupies the island's central high plateau and owes its protected status to its Canarian *laurasilva* forest – the largest and most complete known example of the species left in the world. *Laurasilva* (a woodland of ferns, laurels and heath trees) thrives on damp conditions and much of the forest is cloaked in a veil of mist year-round. During the winter it is cold and damp, but in summer it dries to an extent where forest fires are a hazard. The trails within the Garajonay are very popular with walkers and there are two information centres: at La Laguna Grande (see page 112) and Juego de Bolas (see above).

The highest point on the island, El Alto de Garajonay (Mount Garajonay), at 1,487m, falls within the park and on a good day offers excellent views.

VALLEHERMOSO

This compact village hugging the valley side is a fine sight when approached

The church of Vallehermoso. The village lies beneath El Roque Cano (the Dog Rock)

from the TF112 to the north. At the entrance to Vallehermoso is a particularly artistic children's playground. The giant sculpture of three curvaceous ladies with headdresses would grace many a modern art museum. Vallehermoso has a lively centre with two bustling *tapas* bars, from which old houses rise up to the church.

42km northwest of San Sebastián.

San Sebastián

Your first view of La Gomera, from the ferry, will be of the island capital, San Sebastián. If the fishing fleet is in, and if the long-term restorations to beach and harbour have been finished, you may well like it. San Sebastián is famous for its Columbus associations (he sailed from here in 1492) but makes light of it – there are few exhibits or memorabilia of this era.

IGLESIA DE LA ASUNCIÓN
(Church of the Assumption)

This ancient church on Calle del Medio is the one site in San Sebastián that we know Columbus visited. Records tell us he prayed here in 1492, even though most of the present church dates from the 16th century. It's a fine building, with beautiful woodwork, notably the ceiling and the balcony above the entrance doors. Note, too, the mural depicting the town's defence against an English fleet in 1734.

A little further along Calle del Medio is the Casa Colón/Casa Columbina. The veracity of a Columbus connection is doubtful here, but occasionally the house stages Columbus exhibitions.

San Sebastián, dwarfed by its surroundings

PARADOR CONDE DE LA GOMERA (Parador of the Count of Gomera)

Step into the beautiful *parador* courtyard and peeping out from behind the luxuriant plants you'll see portraits of Columbus and other contemporary historical worthies. Here, more than anywhere in San Sebastián, the spirit of the age is conjured up. It comes as something of a disappointment to learn that this state hotel was built in 1973. It is a glorious reproduction of a typical aristocratic island mansion, but has no historical pedigree whatsoever (see pages 170–1).
Lomo de la Horca (signposted from the harbour).

POZO DE COLÓN (Well of Columbus)

It is known that Columbus's men took water from La Gomera to the New World and as the hole in the ground here is the nearest well to the harbour, logic has it that this must be 'the well that baptised America'. The well is only accessible through the old Casa del Pozo de la Aguada (House of the Well), formerly the Custom House and now the Tourist Office.
Calle del Medio (tel: 87 01 55). Open: Monday to Friday, 8.30am–2pm and 4.30–6pm; Saturday, 10am–noon.

TORRE DEL CONDE (Tower of the Count)

This sturdy pink and white brick tower was built in 1447 by the first Count of Gomera, Hernán Peraza the Elder. His namesake son became something of a tyrant and was killed by Guanches at the Degollada de Peraza (see below), reputedly after being lured to a love nest nearby. His wife, Beatriz de Bobadilla,

The ferry terminal on San Sebastián harbour

was notorious throughout Spanish royal circles for her promiscuity and, like her husband, was also capable of brutal behaviour. She is said to have entertained Columbus in the tower and there are rumours of an affair.
The tower was also used for storing riches from the New World en route to Spain. It is expected to open sometime in the future as an exhibition area.
Next to the harbour front.

Near by

LOS ROQUES

The main southern route from San Sebastián (TF713) passes a number of outstanding volcanic plug rock formations. The first and most interesting is the Roque del Sombrero (8km from town), which actually resembles a pointed Chinese hat, peaking at 663m. After 16km there is a spectacular, if windy *mirador* at the Degollada (Pass) de Peraza (see above). Looming above it is the mightiest of the rocks, Roque de Agando (1,250m). There are three more notable *roques* on the other side of the road: from east to west, Carmen (1,140m), Zarcita (1,235m) and Ojila (1,169m).

Southern La Gomera

The south of La Gomera accommodates the island's two tourist resorts, Playa de Santiago and Valle Gran Rey. Yet both are relatively isolated and would hardly even register on the average Canarian holiday development scale. The Valle Gran Rey was, until recently, only known by a few hippy-types, whereas the hotel complex at Playa de Santiago attracts a monied clientèle. What effect the new airport will have on these places is yet to be seen.

EL CERCADO/CHIPUDE

These neighbouring hamlets, divided by a ridge, could almost be twins. Chipude is the more handsome of the pair, enjoying a splendid setting against the foot of the table-top mountain known as La Fortaleza (1,243m).

In El Cercado you can see the craft of *alfareria* – pottery made from the dark Gomeran earth without a wheel (see pages 142–3).
El Cercado is 37km northwest of San Sebastián. Chipude is 39km northwest of San Sebastián.

LA LAGUNA GRANDE

The 'big lagoon' has long gone, but this is a popular meeting point for walkers, as it is an entrance point to the Garajonay National Park (see page 109). There is an information office and a log cabin, which in winter has a roaring fire. For non-walkers there is also a children's playground and a barbecue area.
29km northwest of San Sebastián. Open: Tuesday to Saturday, 9am–4.30pm. On Fridays, walking tours depart from here. Reservations are essential (tel: 80 09 93, Juego de Bolas office).

PLAYA DE SANTIAGO

The stony beach here is in the infancy of development, with a handful of bars and restaurants lining its new promenade. At the far end is a small fishing port. Above the beach, the

Primitive in style and primitive in creation, the pottery at El Cercado is shaped by hand without the aid of the potter's wheel

Hotel Tecina is very much in the vanguard of Gomeran tourism. With some 342 rooms to offer, this is a veritable giant, but it has not abused its power. The architecture is vernacular and rooms are in village-style bungalows, set in beautifully laid out grounds. Excursions and walking tours may be organised here through the Gomera Safari travel agency. Notice the colourful statues outside the hotel. The grinning *conquistador* is understandably pleased with himself, but the native Indian (presumably meant to be a Guanche) looks as if he would be far more at home in North America. *34km southwest of San Sebastián.*

VALLE GRAN REY

The origin of the name 'Valley of the Great King' goes back to Guanche times, but this is still a place fit for royalty. There is only one road into the valley and it is arguably the most beautiful on the island. Towards the bottom the views to the emerald green slopes on the far side are breathtaking,

The precipitous slopes of Valle Gran Rey; the valley floor is rich in palms and bananas

LOS ORGANOS

Los Órganos (the organ pipes) is an extraordinary 200m-wide formation of slender, tightly packed basalt columns. Some of these reach over 80m high and they do, indeed, resemble giant petrified church organ pipes.

Los Organos is located just off the north coast and may only be viewed from the sea. Boats depart from Valle de Gran Rey, Playa de Santiago and San Sebastián. For further details contact the tourist information office in San Sebastián.

with row upon row of little white houses perched precariously on steep terraces.

At the valley bottom, the road splits – left to the port, right to La Playa Calera. The latter is the only sandy beach on the island and is showing signs of small-scale development. The pretty village of La Calera lies behind the resort.

En route to the Valle Gran Rey, stop at the Mirador del Santo at Arure (10km north of La Calera). It is one of the finest viewpoints on the island. *Valle Gran Rey is 52km west of San Sebastián.*

Vallehermoso Walk

This walk combines Gomeran landscapes of lush valleys in deep ravines, overlooked by volcanic rocks, with a charming reservoir. It is suitable for any age and fitness level, though the hill is reasonably steep, and much of it could be followed in an ordinary car. *Allow 1–1½ hours.*

Start in the centre of Vallehermoso and follow the road uphill out of town, to the left of the Bar Rte Amaya.

1 ROQUE CANO

The large 'Canine Rock' which protrudes 650m into the sky and dominates the view is named after its resemblance to a canine tooth. Like so many other volcanic outcrops on the island, it is merely the central volcanic lava plug – the rest of the cone has long been eroded away.

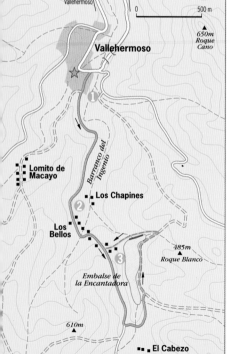

As you continue to climb, look back for fine views of Vallehermoso and its church. Down to your left, the abundance of the lush valley is clear. Bananas, palm trees, sugar cane, orange groves and vines all jostle for space. *Continue your climb up the hill, which becomes steeper and rounds a bend.*

2 THE VALLEY OF 1001 PALMS

It is doubtful whether anyone has really counted the trees here, but as many are on tap for Gomera's famous palm-honey (see page 163), it is possible. Look for metal cups attached to the trunks, catching the 'honey' (palm sap). Metal bands on the trees keep the ants at bay.

Whatever the number of trees, this valley is a splendid sight, particularly in the late afternoon, as the sun comes directly down into it.

After about 20 minutes' walking you will see the dam wall holding back the reservoir.

It is easy to see why Vallehermoso ('beautiful valley') is so named

3 EMBALSE DE LA ENCANTADORA

Despite its function, supplying water to the village and valleys below, this reservoir has a natural, almost ornamental look, hence its romantic name – the Lake of the Enchanted Lady. Ducks bob on its surface and there is a statue of a man – perhaps a Guanche – stranded on a tiny island with just a pole for company. Walk all the way around the reservoir. You'll probably meet a goat or two en route, tethered and grazing. As you complete the circle, cross the metal bridge and (if you don't suffer from vertigo) look down the sheer wall of the dam, trickling water into the valley.
Walk back down the hill and take the right turn downhill.

Down here is a very ramshackle smallholding of goats, chickens, pigeons and rabbits. Don't mind the barking dog (as long as he is attached to his tether!). This descends all the way to the foot of the dam where the running water forms a small stream. You can cross this to the orange groves on the other side but you can go no further.
Return to the main road and descend back down into the village.

EL SILBO

Due to the communication difficulties imposed by the landscape, the Gomerans have developed a unique language known as *el silbo* (the whistle). This is no ordinary whistling; it has real modulation, vocabulary and stentorian volume. It is said that some *silbadores* can communicate from up to 5km away. With the advent of telecommunications and the decline of traditional values, practitioners are becoming rare. The gardener at the *parador* may well demonstrate *silbo* for you; otherwise join the tourist show at Las Rosas restaurant (see page 167).

La Palma

*L*a Palma is quite unlike the other, smaller Canary islands and in many ways stands superior to its larger cousins. It is known throughout the Canaries as La Isla Verde (the Green Island), due to its comparative abundance of water. For the farmers this means profitable banana, tobacco and avocado crops; for tourists it means the most tropical and, many would argue, the most beautiful landscape in the archipelago. This natural beauty is enhanced by the islanders' homes and gardens, often said to be the best kept in the Canaries.

La Palma has a relatively prosperous history. Its capital, Santa Cruz de la Palma, was one of only three Spanish ports allowed to trade with the Americas for a period in the 16th century, and even today its aristocratic past is visible.

The island doesn't excel in beach holidays. With just a handful of black beaches and its isolation from the major islands, it attracts only a handful of tourists in search of peace and natural beauty. Their main aim is the Caldera de Taburiente – a massive crater formed some 400,000 years ago by an earth-shattering explosion, subsequently smoothed and greened by nature into an outstanding beauty spot now enjoying

Spanish National Park status. By contrast, the most recent volcanic activity in the Canaries also happened on the island, in 1971. You can still feel the heat beneath your feet.

Two more features help explain the island's dramatic natural appeal. In relation to its surface area it is claimed to be the tallest island in the world. And if you reach the summit (at 2,426m) you will see a gleaming, white astrophysical observation station, which would look right at home on the moon. For La Palma also boasts the clearest, darkest sky in the northern hemisphere.

Cultivating the slopes near Hoya Grande

LA PALMA

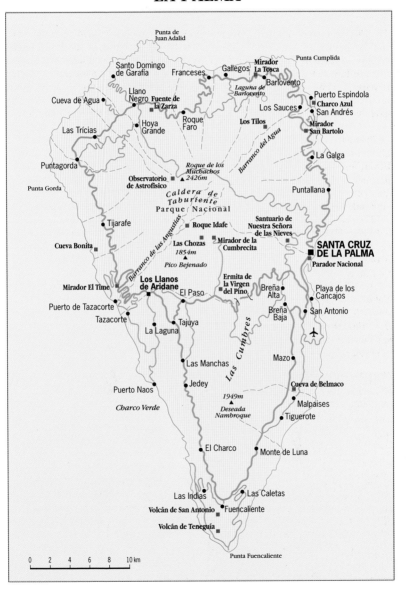

Punta de
Juan Adalid

Santo Domingo
de Garafía
Franceses
Gallegos
**Mirador
La Tosca**
Punta Cumplida

*Laguna de
Barlovento*
Barlovento

Llano
Negro
**Fuente de
la Zarza**
Cueva de Agua
Puerto Espindola
■ **Charco Azul**
Los Sauces
San Andrés

Hoya
Grande
Roque
Faro
Los Tilos
**Mirador
San Bartolo**

Las Trícias
Barranco del Agua
La Galga

Puntagorda
*Roque de los
Muchachos*
▲ *2426m*

Punta Gorda
**Observatorio
de Astrofísico**
Puntallana

*Caldera de
Taburiente*
Parque Nacional

Tijarafe
■ **Roque Idafe**
**Santuario de
Nuestra Señora
de las Nieves**
■

Cueva Bonita ■
Las Chozas
1854m
▲
**Mirador de la
Cumbrecita**
**SANTA CRUZ
DE LA PALMA** ■
Parador Nacional

Barranco de las Angustias
Pico Bejenado

Mirador El Time ■
**Los Llanos
de Aridane** ■
El Paso
**Ermita de
la Virgen
del Pino**
Breña
Alta
Playa de los
Cancajos

Puerto de Tazacorte
Tajuya
Breña
Baja
San Antonio

Tazacorte
La Laguna
✈

Las Manchas
Las Cumbres
Mazo

Puerto Naos
Jedey
Cueva de Belmaco ■

Charco Verde
1949m
▲
*Deseada
Nambroque*
■ Malpaises
Tiguerote

El Charco
Monte de Luna

Las Indias
Las Caletas

Volcán de San Antonio ●**Fuencaliente**

Volcán de Teneguía ■

Punta Fuencaliente

0   2   4   6   8   10 km

Northern La Palma

San Andrés aside, the northern villages of La Palma are unexceptional, and a tour of the whole northern loop can be a tiring experience. However, if the weather is clear, it is worth making the journey to the Roque de los Muchachos, which passes some of the island's most dramatic scenery and ends in spectacular style, peering into the Caldera de Taburiente.

LOS TILOS

Los Tilos (the lime trees) is a damp ancient *laurasilva* forest of limes, laurels, myrtles and ferns. Water flows so thick and fast here, down the Barranco del Agua, that a hydroelectric plant (the only one in the Canary Islands) has been constructed. There is a picnic area and a visitor centre is planned.
29.5km north of Santa Cruz.

PUNTAGORDA

This sparsely inhabited, straggling agricultural settlement lacks any real centre. However, the flower and vegetable fields around here are pretty, particularly in spring, when the pink almond trees bloom.
28km north of Los Llanos de Aridane.

ROQUE DE LOS MUCHACHOS

At 2,426m this is the highest point on the island, perched on the edge of the

The lush green valley of Los Tilos

Caldera de Taburiente (see pages 124–5). The road which leads here is tortuous, scenic (lunar-like in places) and passes through clouds before bursting back into sunlight near the top. This peak is always cold and in winter is often covered in snow (in very bad weather the road is cut off). Having braved the journey, there are wonderful views down into the *caldera* (crater) and near by are the intriguing white domes of the Observatorio de Astrofísico (Astrophysical Observatory) opened in 1985 (see pages 120–1).
44km northwest of Santa Cruz.

NORTHERN MIRADORES

There are two fine *miradores* to look out for while touring the north. Just north of La Galga (19km north of Santa Cruz), look for the signpost Mirador La Montaña. Stop by the small church of Ermita de San Bartolomé for a view along the east coast, then drive uphill to the Mirador San Bartolo, which has panoramic views inland.

At the very top of the island, just west of Barlovento, turn right towards Gallegos. After just over 1km the Mirador La Tosca gives views along the north coast. Look down to your right to a curious colony of dragon trees (see pages 90).

Holy of Holies – the glittering image of Our Lady of the Snows

SAN ANDRÉS Y LOS SAUCES

The top half of this twinned village, Los Sauces, is a modern agricultural centre of little interest. Take the road down through the dense banana plantations to San Andrés, where you will find a charming square shared by a 17th-century church, well-tended gardens and a popular fish restaurant. From here old houses tumble down the steep cobbled hill towards the sea.

Near San Andrés is Charco Azul ('the blue pool'), a pleasantly situated semi-natural lido with refreshments.
San Andrés is 28km north of Santa Cruz.

SANTUARIO DE NUESTRA SEÑORA DE LAS NIEVES (Sanctuary of Our Lady of the Snows)

This is the most sacred spot on the island, though curiously 'the snows' refer not to the island peaks but to a 4th-century miracle, when the Virgin appeared during snow in August in Rome. The focus of attention is the 14th-century terracotta figure of the Virgin, the island's patron saint and probably the oldest image in all the islands. There is some fine gold- and silver-work in the 17th-century chapel which houses the figure, and the restaurant in the square also makes this a pleasant stop.

Every five years (in August) the figure is brought down to Santa Cruz in a grand procession known as La Bajada de la Virgen (the descent of the Virgin). Great festivities follow and if you intend visiting the island during this period, be sure to book well ahead. The next *Bajada* is in the year 2000.
3½km west of Santa Cruz.

LA PALMA OBSERVATORY

Why on earth is the most important space observatory in the northern hemisphere sited on an obscure Canary Island? The answer is that La Palma provides a combination of geographical, topographical and meteorological factors which are perfect for star-gazing.

The remoteness of the island and its lack of development means that the observatory (El Observatorio del Roque de los Muchachos) is free from distracting artificial light; the shape of the mountain and the prevailing winds mean the airflow here is comparatively undisturbed; and the site is above the clouds (which trap dust and moisture) for the vast majority of the year. Put all these together and it means that extremely faint stars and galaxies, mind-boggling distances away, can be observed with the utmost clarity.

The observatory complex was inaugurated in 1985 and is host to a number of different international organisations. The largest observatory is operated by the English Royal Greenwich Observatory and includes the William Herschel telescope. This is the third largest in the world, but has the advantage of its La Palma site

and the quality of its instrumentation over its two larger rivals, and is therefore probably the finest window on the universe in the world.

If you would like to see inside the complex, tours are occasionally given in summer (tel: 40 55 00 for details). Don't expect to look through a working telescope, however. 'Telescope time' here is fought over by professional astronomers from all over the world and is usually three-times over subscribed.

Disappointingly for romantics, the popular image of the astronomer with his eye to the lens, wrapped in scarves to keep warm, is well out of date. Eyes are rarely put to lenses at La Palma and the telescopes are remote-controlled from computer consoles, while operators sit in warm, comfortable rooms.

The William Herschel telescope and its housing, high above the clouds

Santa Cruz

*A*rchitecturally, Santa Cruz is one of the most harmonious and handsome small towns in the archipelago. Its wealth from trade with the Americas may have passed, but its well-preserved buildings reflect a comfortable sense of prosperity. Tourism has hardly touched the town. There are two low-key museums here, and a *parador*, though you could walk past the latter and not even know it existed. But the town has plenty to offer the visitor in terms of authentic Spanish colonial atmosphere and by night the Avenida Marítima becomes a lively promenade of pavement bars and cafés.

AVENIDA MARÍTIMA

Santa Cruz has one of the least spoiled seafronts of any town in the Canaries. At its southern end is a bizarre dragon tree with four 'heads' peering out on long 'necks', set at 90° to the main trunk. The *parador* (see pages 170–1), with its dark wooden galleries, is an appetiser for the splendid, traditionally balconied houses further along. Until recently these were painted dark green and white. Now they are a pastel rainbow of blues and greens, yellows, browns and pinks.

A little further along is the Castillo de Santa Catalina, built in the 16th century, though much altered in later years. Its entrance is to the rear, but it is presently closed to the public.

CALLE O'DALY

Running parallel to the Avenida Marítima, the cobbled Calle O'Daly reflects the 17th- and 18th-century wealth of the town, boasting several handsome merchants' houses. The street is named after an Irish banana merchant who settled on the island (towards the northern end it changes name to Calle Real). Walking from south to north look out for nos 42, 38, 28, 26 and 24. Of special note is no 22, built in the first half of the 17th century as the Palacio Salazar, and now housing the tourist office. After passing through the Plaza de España (see below), visit the casino at no 7 (or 15, depending on which numbering you follow). This building, with a mix of Moorish and Colonial architecture, is now a social club. Just below here is the delightful small square of Placeta de Borreo.

At the very end of the street is the surprising sight of a full-size galleon. It is a replica of Columbus's flagship, the *Santa María*, made of concrete. Columbus never actually called here but the island did become wealthy on American trade and this is also a monument to the town's 19th-century

Canarian houses on Avenida Maritima, decorated with Spanish colonial-style balconies

Plaza de España, the jewel in the crown of Santa Cruz

shipbuilders. Within it is a small naval museum.

Tourist information office, Palacio Salazar (tel: 41 21 06). Open: Monday to Saturday, 8.30am–1pm and 5pm–7pm. Santa María naval museum open: Monday to Friday, 10am–1pm and 4pm–7pm; Saturday, 10am–1pm. Admission charge.

MUSEO INSULAR (Island Museum)

The island's historical and ethnographical collection is housed in the 16th-century convent of San Francisco, which is located within the grounds of the church of the same name. This has been closed for some time, undergoing long-term restoration. Ask at the tourist office for opening details.

Calle San Francisco, off Calle O'Daly.

PLAZA DE ESPAÑA

This fine ensemble of historic buildings is the heart of the capital. Look inside the 16th-century Iglesia del Salvador (Church of the Saviour). The ceiling is a splendid example of *mudéjar* (see pages 154–5) woodwork and its gothic arched sacristy is also notable. Its treasures include a painted altarpiece and a remarkable silver cross in a rear chapel.

Adjacent to the church is a fine drinking fountain. The beautiful building on the corner of the plaza is now the home of the Spanish Open University.

The *ayuntamiento* (town hall) was built in 1569 with a Renaissance arcade and a fine Colonial interior; it was once the Cardinal's palace. Step inside during office hours to admire the colourful mural by Mariano de Cossío on the stairway and the outstanding carved panelling ceiling.

Iglesia del Salvador. Open: daily, 8.30am–1pm and 4pm–8.30pm.

Southern La Palma

*T*his southern loop of La Palma includes the most picturesque villages and, from Fuencaliente to Los Llanos de Aridane, the most scenic driving stretch of the island. Pine forests sweep down the hillside to pretty roadside hamlets, while superb coastal views open out ahead. The mountains loom ever closer and the Mirador de la Cumbrecita, the climax of the drive, provides unforgettable views into the Caldera de Taburiente.

FUENCALIENTE

This neat village is famous for its two volcanoes and its wine, both of which can easily be sampled by taking a walk around the volcanoes (see pages 126–7), then visiting the *bodegas* (wine cellars). *33km south of Santa Cruz. Bodegas de Teneguía (tel: 44 70 78). Open: Monday to Friday, 9am–2pm and 3pm–5pm (winter); 8am–1pm (summer).*

LOS LLANOS DE ARIDANE

It's easy to drive along the dual carriageway that bypasses Los Llanos and completely miss the old centre of town. Instead, turn right here (heading from Santa Cruz) and you will find a charming plaza with an early 16th-century church, Iglesia de los Remedios, a typically Canarian *ayuntamiento* (town hall) and café tables and chairs spreading beneath ancient Indian laurel trees.

Step behind the church and there are more fine old houses and a view of the mountains.

Near by, the Mirador El Time offers

The humbling power of Mother Nature; peering into Caldera de Taburiente, one of the world's deepest craters

spectacular views back along the south coast from an almost sheer elevation of 594m.

Los Llanos de Aridane is 32km west of Santa Cruz.

MAZO

Saturday afternoon and Sunday morning markets bring tourists and locals to this small village. Do look into the fine 16th-century Iglesia de San Blás which has a number of 16th-century statues and a fine high altar. Just outside the village on the road to Hoyo de Maza is the highly regarded pottery workshop of El Molino (see page 142–3).

Some 4km south of Mazo, Guanche inscriptions may be found in the Cueva (Cave) de Belmaco.

Mazo is 15km south of Santa Cruz.

PARQUE NACIONAL DE LA CALDERA DE TABURIENTE (National Park of the Crater of Taburiente)

The *caldera*, or crater, which comprises this protected area measures 9km across at its widest point and has a circumference of 28km. It was formed some 400,000 years ago in a massive explosion, and since then the elements have gouged the crater even deeper (down to 900m) and have turned it into one of the most green and beautiful places in the archipelago.

There is only one surfaced road into the National Park, and that is from the south, leading to the spectacular Mirador de la Cumbrecita. There is an information kiosk here and this is also where free guided walks start (pre-booking essential). There are more views from Lomo de Las Chozas, a pleasant walk 1km due west. Serious walkers also enter the park from its southwest corner via the

Barranco de las Angustias.

This *barranco* (ravine) was the last bastion of La Palma's Guanches and the great monolith known as Roque Idafe was a sacred point to them.

Mirador de la Cumbrecita is 30km west of Santa Cruz (tel: 48 60 00).

TAZACORTE

The upper part of Tazacorte retains much of its old character and is pleasantly laid out, with a promenade looking over dense green banana plantations down towards Puerto de Tazacorte. The focal point is a raised plaza where the locals sit under a bougainvillea-decked pergola next to a pretty church.

The fishing port of Puerto de Tazacorte, 3km to the north, has a black sand beach served by a handful of bars and restaurants.

The west coast's largest resort is Puerto Naos, 11km south of Tazacorte. This has a much larger beach and on it the 300-bed, 4-star Sol Palma hotel – by far the biggest and most luxurious accommodation on the island.

Tazacorte is 38km west of Santa Cruz.

Banana plantations below Tazacorte

La Palma Volcanoes Walk

This walk shows you two of La Palma's volcanoes (one still warm!) in a spectacular coastal setting. The walk around Volcán de San Antonio is a level 30-minute circle open to everyone, though it does become slightly vertiginous on the far side. The walk down to Teneguía is rather steep but you have the option of driving down to it. The walk up to the rim of Volcán de Teneguía is short but reasonably strenuous and should definitely not be attempted in windy weather. *Allow 1½–2 hours' total walking time if you descend all the way from Fuencaliente to Volcán de Teneguía on foot – arrange (in the Bar Parada) for a taxi to collect you at the bottom.*

To get to the Volcán de San Antonio look out for the small sign on the main road in the middle of Fuencaliente opposite the Bar Parada. It's a 10-minute walk or a two-minute drive to the crater car park. Follow the directional arrow that leads you anti-clockwise on a narrow path around the rim of the volcano.

1 VOLCÁN DE SAN ANTONIO

This 657m-high volcano erupted over the course of 66 days in 1667 and is now starting to look mature, with pine trees on its lower inner slopes and foliage higher up. To your right, sloping down towards the sea, is the village of Las Indias. As you round the edge of the volcano there are excellent views back to Fuencaliente, framed by the green hills above.

The volcano drops away steeply to the sea and below are wonderful views of Volcán de Teneguía. On a sunny day the volcano reveals its shades of reds and purples but even when plain

The rim of the 300-year old Volcán de San Antonio

matt-black, it's a fine sight against the blue Atlantic Ocean. If you visit in summer the space in between the two volcanoes is covered in leafy vines, bright lime-green against the black lava-fields. The farmers of Fuencaliente have taken advantage of the natural disaster to cultivate wines which thrive on this soil. *Just before you complete the circle around the rim, a path drops away to your right. Follow this, then follow the winding paths that snake downhill to Teneguía, which is clearly visible. Head for the car park.*
Alternatively, if you want a shorter walk, return to your car, continue driving downhill and take the sharp left turn towards Los Quemados. Take the track signposted 'Teneguía 1971', then take the first turning right, which takes you down to the car park. The ascent to the rim of the volcano takes 20–30 minutes.

2 VOLCÁN DE TENEGUÍA

This is the youngest volcano in the archipelago, having erupted for 25 days as recently as 1971. It's said that the fountain of lava cascaded 200m into the air, and it produced the equivalent of 2 million lorry-loads of lava, but no-one was hurt. Hot gases still emanate through the crater walls and the ground is warm. Don't worry: the volcano is receding. Lava-streams spread down to the coast, towards the lighthouse and saltpans, and have actually extended the island by a few metres.

El Hierro

*E*l Hierro is the most westerly, the smallest and the least known of all the Canary Islands. As if to underline the point, Las Puntas (see page 131) is the home of what is claimed to be the world's smallest hotel. Such solitude and lack of pretensions inevitably draw a small following of visitors who come here for the walking and peace and quiet which is offered by the island.

The history of the island is also fairly uneventful. The *Herreños* were the only Canarians to surrender peaceably to the Spanish invaders. Unfortunately they did not foresee that the *conquistadores* would then sell them into slavery. In 1493 Columbus may have called here during his second voyage to the New World; since then not a lot has happened.

The great natural feature of El Hierro is the bay of El Golfo (the Gulf). This is thought to be the rim of a massive crater, half of which is submerged and half of which rises dramatically to over 1,000m. El Hierro has other natural scenery to rival the best in the Canaries: splendid

EL HIERRO

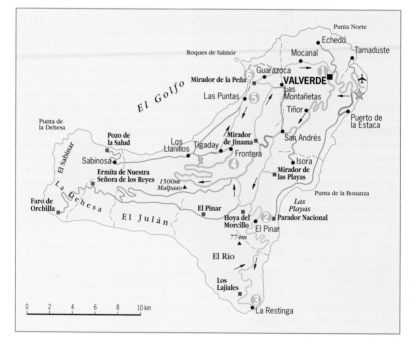

pine forests; strange, twisted juniper trees unique to the island; sheer mountain walls and spectacular *miradores*.

There is, however, a shortage of accommodation. The *parador* would seem the most comfortable choice, but it is isolated, even by El Hierro standards. If you intend staying overnight, book ahead (see page 171).

Touring can be frustrating. El Hierro may only be 24 by 27km at its maximum dimensions, but the configuration of its roads means that a good deal of backtracking is inevitable. The west of the island can only be explored along slow and bumpy dirt tracks and the south coast is all but inaccessible.

Right: Candelaria Church, Frontera
Below: the harbour at La Restinga

EL HIERRO

■Valverde
.Frontera
Sabínosa•
El Pinar•
•La Restinga

El Hierro Drive

This tour is designed for visitors with just one day on the island and takes in virtually all the island highlights. For the route see the El Hierro map on page 128. *Allow 5–6 hours.*

From the airport follow the winding road inland for 7km.

1 VALVERDE

The island capital's only sign of importance is the sturdy late 18th-century church, Iglesia de la Concepción, that once gave protection against corsairs. Aside from a small ornamental plaza and a tourist office, it is essentially just a village. Surprisingly there are two small museums here. The Exposición de Fondos Etnográficos y Arqueológicos is above the tourist office and exhibits old domestic implements and tools, and local folk costume; The Museo Juan Padrón is a private house with a collection of local antiquities at Calle Previsor Magdalena 8.

Head south through San Andrés and turn left towards El Pinar.

2 EL PINAR

Gently rolling countryside of beautiful pine forests makes up this area with the small settlement of the same name at its heart. Stop at the Mirador de las Playas for a wonderful view of the bay of Las Playas. The building with the red-tiled roof is the island *parador* (see page 129). *Continue south for 13km.*

3 LA RESTINGA

This fishing port is marked by an ugly seawall which does at least create calm swimming conditions. Adventurous German tourists are cultivating La Restinga into something of a frontier resort. As you head along this road note the strange rope-lava landscape just north of La Restinga.
Return to El Pinar and turn off left onto the secondary road towards Frontera. Turn left again as it rejoins the main road.

4 FRONTERA

As the road descends to the coast, fine views of El Golfo (see page 128) appear. Tantalising views also appear of the church of Frontera. From afar it seems tiny and hopelessly isolated against the great green-grey mountain wall that makes up one side of El Golfo. But on closer inspection this is just a small belltower built on to a volcanic cone – the church itself is on the road below.

Frontera is the island's wine-growing centre and large deserted antique *lagares* (wine-presses) may occasionally be seen on the hillsides.

El Golfo from Mirador de Jinama. The village lies on the rim of half a volcanic crater, the other half of which is submerged beneath the sea

---

> ***Tourist information office,*** *Calle Dr Quintero 11, (tel: 55 03 02). Open: Monday to Saturday, 9am–2.30pm.*
> ***Valverde museums:*** *both have unpredictable opening times; enquire at the tourist information office.*

Continue on the TF912 to Tigaday, then turn right to head downhill towards the sea.

5 LAS PUNTAS

Aside from the 'world's smallest hotel' (see page 128) by the remains of the old harbour, there's not much at Las Puntas, but it's a pleasant drive down to the sea with its rocky outcrops. Almost directly above to the right is the Mirador de la Peña (see below).
Backtrack all the way beyond Frontera and after 20km turn left onto a minor road to the Mirador de Jinama. Enjoy the view here, continue and turn left onto the main road.

6 MIRADOR DE LA PEÑA

This superb enclosed viewing point is the work of César Manrique (see pages 66–7) and bears his hallmarks of local construction style and materials, excellent food and a peaceful atmosphere. The cliff on which it is perched falls almost sheer, 600m to the sea, offering the best view of El Golfo on the island.

Note the strange native *sabina* (juniper) tree outside the *mirador*, grotesquely twisted by the fierce winds, yet still alive. A small forest of these exists at El Sabinar in the west of the island.
Return 8km east to Valverde and turn left to the airport.

MYTHOLOGY

All distant isles attract myths and legends and the hoariest island legend of all – Atlantis – is often connected with the Canaries. Plato described Atlantis as lying to the west of Gibraltar. Some 10,000 years before his time, so he wrote, it had been sent to the bottom of the ocean by earthquakes and tidal waves, until only seven mountain tops remained above the waters. Could this be the Canaries? Atlantis, a happy and wealthy land, also sounds rather like the Fortunate Islands, as the Canaries were described

Plato's timescale was also inaccurate, as even the youngest islands are some two million years old.

And what should we make of the 'eighth Canary Island' – San Borondón? The island was named after St Brendan (or Brandan), a 6th-century Irish monk who sailed for seven years in search of the island where the saints were reincarnated. According to 16th-century Portuguese navigators, San Borondón lay 2–300 sea miles northwest of La Palma. By Canarian standards it was huge; 422km from north to south and 149km from east to west. Coincidentally, the island also had seven cities.

The legend continues that after seven years on the island, Brendan and his monks were told to leave by an angel. After yet another seven years, just as he was despairing of sighting land, an island (perhaps the same island) appeared. But immediately after the monks had celebrated mass the land rumbled; they beat a hasty retreat back to their boat and the island sank.

in antiquity – a land of plenty, of eternal springtime, with 'fertile soil and crops and fruit without working'.

Unfortunately for the romantics, this story does not match current theories suggesting that volcanoes created, rather than destroyed the land.

Apparently, when the weather conditions are right, you can look out northwest from La Palma and see the high mountain peaks of San Borondón – but don't book your next holiday there just yet!

GETTING AWAY
FROM IT ALL

> *My footsteps always remained in the sands. The fleeting outline of my feet was perfect and unchanging. I breathed the pure iodine of the Atlantic.*
>
> **CÉSAR MANRIQUE,**
> *Lanzarote artist, designer and environmentalist.*

Beyond the Resorts

Getting away from it all need never present a problem in the Canary Islands. This is self-evident for those travelling to the quiet islands of El Hierro, La Palma and La Gomera, but even on the major resort islands it is true. The very fact that mega-resorts have been built on the south coasts of Tenerife and Gran Canaria means that tourism is contained within well-defined limits.

ADVENTURE EXCURSIONS

Jeep safaris

If you want to get off the main roads and see the landscape, you might consider joining a jeep safari. The best of these explore tracks which most hire cars fear (or are simply unable) to tread. There

are drawbacks, however. The back of a jeep is hard, cramped and particularly uncomfortable in inclement weather. It's also impossible for a tour leader to give a running commentary. Some jeep safaris let their clients drive. If you want to try your four-wheel drive skills this may be fine, but you may not be so happy being driven at high speeds over rough ground by a novice whom you have never met before! Jeep excursions are available on all the islands (except El Hierro) through a number of operators and are widely advertised.

Boat safaris

Boat trips (or 'safaris') are widely available from most of the larger tourist resorts and can be a good way to see a different aspect of an island. However, you should always find out what you are letting yourself in for in advance. Do you really want 'free' wine and 'pirate games' or would you prefer coastal views and undisturbed relaxation?

A bewildering variety of craft is available – sailing yachts, large motor launches, small motor launches, glass-hulled catamarans and the antique *Nostramo*, built in 1919.

If you would prefer to skipper your own course it's easy to charter a boat

Getting to grips with the wilder side of the Canaries on a 4x4 Jeep Safari

Bottle-nosed dolphins are a common sight in Tenerife waters

from pleasure marinas or yacht clubs (club náuticos). See pages 156–61 for the major centres.

The most interesting boat safaris depart from southern Tenerife in search of dolphins and whales off the southwest coast. Some 200 short-finned pilot whales live and breed just offshore and these can normally be seen together with bottle-nosed dolphins.

Submarine excursions, which depart from Puerto Mogán, Gran Canaria and Las Galletas, Tenerife should be taken for what they are – pure gimmicks. These are authentic miniature submarines and it is undoubtedly a novel experience but, aside from specially placed wrecks and a few fish, there is little to see – and they are very expensive.

HORSE-RIDING

This is a near-perfect way to get off the beaten track and offers excursions both inland and sometimes along deserted beaches. All the following establishments offer tuition:

Lanzarote: Lanzarote a Caballo between Yaiza and Mácher (tel: 83 03 14); El Establo, Costa Teguise (tel: 59 04 37).

Gran Canaria: Rancho Park, near Palmitos Parque; Bandama Golf Club Riding School, near Las Palmas (tel: 35 12 90); Maspalomas Oasis Riding School (tel: 76 23 78).

Tenerife: El Rodeo de la Paja, El Ortigal, between La Laguna and La Esperanza, instruction only in Spanish (tel: 25 40 11).

A solitary beach on Fuerteventura with Los Lobos in the background

beaches on Lanzarote are also known for baring it all, though these can get crowded while on Tenerife, Los Gaviotas, next to Playa de las Teresitas, too is a naturist beach.

The beaches on La Graciosa and Los Lobos (see **Islets**, below) are also recommended for escaping the crowds.

ISLETS

Most holiday guides will tell you there are seven Canary Islands – in fact there are 13. The four other tiny islands of Los Lobos (north of Fuerteventura) Isla Graciosa, Montaña Clara and Alegranza are all north of Lanzarote and the two rocky islets of Roque del Oeste and Roque del Este are in the province of Las Palmas.

Regular ferries run to and from Los Lobos and Graciosa. You can walk round Los Lobos in just over two hours. Aside from other curious tourists, you won't see a soul, as no-one lives here. The main attraction is the beach and a pretty lagoon (see pages 54). Don't forget your picnic. By comparison, Graciosa (see pages 70) is positively throbbing. There are two tiny settlements here and you can even stay overnight in a pension. The beach here is superb.

To get to the tiny other island rocks (further north), you will need an accommodating fishing boat. Ask on Graciosa or at Orzola on Lanzarote. Alegranza is approximately half the size of Graciosa, at 10 sq km, and lies 20km off the north coast of Lanzarote. There is a tiny fishing community here but unless you're a bird-watcher you may well wonder why the island was so named (Alegranza means 'joy').

BEACHES

Conventional wisdom suggests that you need a four-wheel drive vehicle to find the away-from-it-all beaches. However, this is not always the case. One of the finest beaches in all the islands, Playa de las Teresitas at Santa Cruz on the main coast road of Tenerife, is quiet for most of the year. Fuerteventura is a beach-bum's paradise, with mile upon mile of golden sands allowing space for everyone. But if you find yourself on a solitary beach, particularly one facing north or west (this applies to all the islands), swim with great caution, if at all. Currents can be treacherous and a number of holidaymakers seeking solitude on the west coast of Fuerteventura have come to grief.

Naturists can take cover among the dunes either at Maspalomas on Gran Canaria or at Corralejo on Fuerteventura. Some of the Papagayo

Montaña Clara (just off Graciosa) is the smallest of all at just 1 sq km. It's also the most spectacular with a 256m high volcano at its heart.

MOUNTAIN BIKES

These are available for hire from most major resorts. Only the very fit will attempt the mountainous inland routes but Lanzarote and Fuerteventura in particular offer a reasonable amount of flat terrain to explore.

On Tenerife, group cycling tours occasionally depart from the Hotel Tigaiga (see below under **Walking** for details).

WALKING

As more and more inquisitive travellers drive hire cars to every corner of each island it soon becomes apparent that the only way to leave the crowds behind is to walk. At first sight the Canaries may not seem ideal for the casual walker. The terrain is often daunting, most islands are not waymarked and there are few walking tour guides to help you. But don't be put off. One of the best-kept secrets on the islands is the free National Park walking tour service provided by ICONA, the Spanish nature conservancy organisation. Just telephone ahead to book your place and you can enjoy an insider's view of some of the finest scenery on Lanzarote (Timanfaya, pages 69, 78–9), Tenerife (Mount Teide, pages 88–9), La Gomera (Garajonay, pages 109) and La Palma (Caldera de Taburiente, pages 124–5). See under individual entries for telephone numbers and meeting points. The National Park information offices on Tenerife, La Gomera and La Palma can also supply maps with footpaths for independent exploration.

Las Cañadas National Park, Tenerife

Walking tours

Surprisingly, there are very few commercial walking tour operators on the islands. 'Ecological Tours', on Gran Canaria, lay on a whole day of three easy treks for walkers of all abilities. The programme varies but usually starts with an introduction to the islands' flora via a gentle walk around the Jardín Canario near Las Palmas; then it's a trek down into the Caldera de Bandama (see pages 48–9) and after lunch a marvellous

scenic walk on one of the island's ancient footpaths near Santa Lucía. Book through Viajes Drago, Edificio Excelsior, Playa del Inglés, tel: 76 64 90.

'Gomera Safari' can be found in the shopping arcade of the Hotel Tecina at Playa Santiago and usually include the picturesque 3–4 hour walk from the Roque de Agando to Benchijigua in their programme (tel: 89 51 00). On Tenerife you can join the German-lead tour group, Wandern mit Gregorio (Walks with Gregorio), who depart from the Hotel Tigaiga, Puerto de la Cruz, on both walking and cycling tours. Call the hotel for details, tel: 38 35 00.

ICONA on Tenerife publish a series of walking maps, detailing up to nine walks per map with directions in several languages (including English) – available free from tourist offices. These are not very detailed, but the trails are waymarked – look out for the rustic wooden *Sendero Turistico* (Tourist Footpath) signs.

Tenerife leads the way in signposting walks and a favourite easy signed walk is the Barranco del Infierno near Adeje (see page 98). There are also plans here and on Gran Canaria to renovate and open up to the public ancient walkways which criss-cross the island.

As a general rule the best walking is always to be found in the north and centre of the islands; the south is usually too hot and too dry.

You'll need stout walking shoes (boots are best) for walks of any length plus water, sunhat and warm clothing if you are walking at high altitudes. Never walk alone and always tell someone when you will be back.

Island walks (above) near Santa Lucia, Gran Canaria, and (left) Las Cañadas, Tenerife

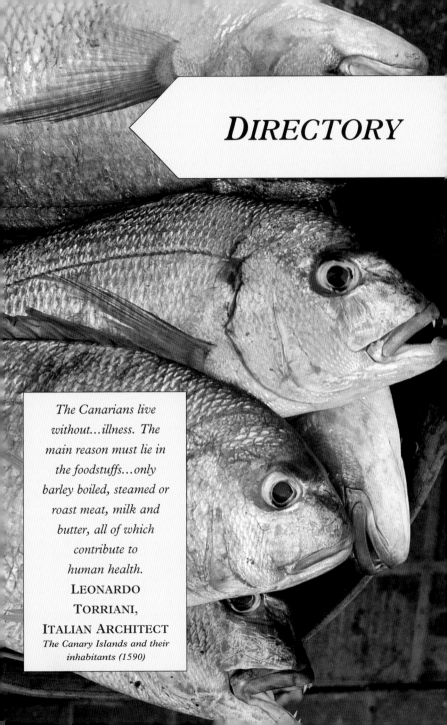

DIRECTORY

The Canarians live without...illness. The main reason must lie in the foodstuffs...only barley boiled, steamed or roast meat, milk and butter, all of which contribute to human health.

LEONARDO TORRIANI, ITALIAN ARCHITECT
The Canary Islands and their inhabitants (1590)

Shopping

*T*he first lesson to learn when shopping in the Canaries is to take all those 'tax-free' and 'duty-free' signs with a pinch of salt. The islands were declared a duty-free zone in 1852 by the Spanish authorities in order to stimulate trade, and ever since then they have retained certain privileges (they are now in fact a 'trade-free' zone, which means they are free of certain import taxes), but these benefits are not necessarily all passed on to the customer.

The luxury goods on which favourable tax rates apply are typically electrical items, cameras, calculators, jewellery, perfume, leather goods and tobacco and spirits. The last two items are certainly bargains but elsewhere there is often little to choose between Canarian retailers and keen international airport duty-free shop prices.

Island goods

There is no doubt that the most satisfying purchases are of those traditional wares made on the islands, sometimes right before your eyes: basketry, wood carvings, pottery, rugs

Up-market shopping on the Avenida de Mesa y López, Las Palmas (Gran Canaria)

and embroidered tableware. You will find *centros artesanías* (craft workshops) throughout the islands but, despite their often rustic nature, their wares are not always cheap. This is because many hours' labour go into them (unlike the machine-produced Far East imports you will see sold on the streets, and in some shops).

Canarian consumables which make interesting presents or tasty souvenirs include *mojo* sauces (see page 163) in small gift packs and wines you can sample in the *bodegas* of Lanzarote or La Palma. Cigars are also a speciality of La Palma, with large Havana-style torpedoes in foil and wooden boxes, making eye-catching and high quality presents. These compare very favourably with the best Cuban cigars.

A bunch of *strelitzias* (see pages 90–1) is an exotic way of saying it with flowers. Florists will box these for you so that they may go straight into the aircraft hold (or you can buy them from street sellers, unboxed, at half the price). *Strelitzias* are hardy travellers and will last for a good number of weeks once cut. You could only really top this with a dragon tree. The full-grown version is not for sale, but seeds are: get them at the shop in Icod de los Vinos next to the tree (see pages 93).

MAIN SHOPPING AREAS

Gran Canaria

Las Palmas is the 'duty-free' mecca of the Canaries. If you can't find the camera you want at a competitive price in the maze of shops between Santa Catalina Parque and the beach, you probably won't find it anywhere. For a classier range of shops including branches of two of Spain's best

department stores, look in the Avenida de Mesa y López. At the other end of town, more department stores and antique shops can be found on Calle Mayor Triana.

The south is not well supplied with shops. The resorts are full of ugly *centro commerciales* (shopping centres), where tat and trinkets generally rule the merchandise roost.

Fuerteventura

The best shopping is to be found in the small shops around the square in Corralejo. Some of these have an ethnic-alternative feel. For a windy day's play on the dunes visit the kite shop.

Lanzarote

Teguise is undoubtedly the island's most interesting shopping experience, on and off market days (see pages 143). Elsewhere, the island lives up to its tasteful arty image with a variety of designer goods and its famous wines are available to sample and buy from *bodegas* in La Geria.

Venerable shop front, Santa Cruz de Tenerife

Tenerife

Santa Cruz runs Las Palmas close for its 'duty-free' goods and the traffic-free central area of Plaza de la Candelaria, Bethencourt Alfonso and Calle del Castillo is popular shopping territory.

Puerto de la Cruz has interesting shops in its centre, and neighbouring La Orotava combines shopping with sightseeing and craft heritage centres (see below and pages 86–7).

Shopping in the south of the island is generally poor.

La Gomera/La Palma/El Hierro

There are few shops on these islands. Look for local wine and liqueurs, palm-honey (see pages 162–3), Guanche-style pottery and handicrafts.

MARKETS

The most colourful shopping in the Canaries takes place on a Sunday morning. Each of the two provincial capitals of Santa Cruz (Tenerife) and Las Palmas (Gran Canaria) stages a bustling *rastro* (flea-market) with a strong African influence. On Lanzarote everyone descends on the Sunday market at Teguise. Eclectic is the only way to describe the range of goods on offer at

these jamborees. The event, particularly at Teguise which is something of a carnival, seems at least as important as the merchandise.

The best daily markets are also held in the capitals. Nuestra Señora de África, at Santa Cruz, is an attraction in its own right, while the sea-front market hall in the Triana area of Las Palmas is the oldest in the Canaries. Gran Canaria also stages notable Sunday markets at San Mateo and Teror.

Other popular markets include the Mercadillo La Havana in La Orotava, Tenerife (on the terrace above the bus station) on Saturdays 9am–3pm which sells antiques, craft and leather goods.

Ask at the tourist office for details of local market days, particularly if you are self-catering.

SHOPS

Normal shop opening hours are Monday to Saturday 9 or 10am to 1 or 2 pm and 4 or 5pm to 7 or 8pm. In the resorts, shops may open longer hours.

All the shops listed below are open during these times unless otherwise stated.

GRAN CANARIA
Galeria de Arte, Fataga
Unusual local pottery and good paintings.
Calle Rios, village centre (tel: 79 82 07).

El Corte Inglés, Las Palmas
The doyen of Spanish department stores; everything from cheap electrical goods to exclusive designer clothes.
Avenida Mesa y López (tel: 26 30 00). Open all day.

A vegetable stall in the Mercado de Nuestra Señora de Africa, Santa Cruz de Tenerife

Tienda de Playa del Inglés, Playa del Inglés

A craft initiative featuring the work of different potters, woodworkers and other artisans.

Avenida de España, turismo office (tel: 77 02 79). Also at Cruz de Tejeda (no telephone).

LA GOMERA
Los Telares, Hermigua

Craft studio where girls weave rugs on ancient looms.

Carretera General (tel: 88 07 81).

LA PALMA
El Molino, Hoya del Mazo

Pottery workshop producing high-quality Guanche-inspired wares.

Carretera Hoya de Mazo. Open Monday to Friday 10am–1pm, 3–5pm (tel: 44 02 13).

LANZAROTE
Fundación César Manrique, Taro de Tahíche

Manrique T-shirts, sweatshirts, posters and prints.

Taro de Tahíche (tel: 81 01 38 and 81 42 70).

Centro Artesanía de Haría, Haría

Textiles, pottery and basket weaving.

Calle Barranco, 4. Closed Monday afternoon.

Centro Natural, Teguise

Alternative lifestyle and beauty products, antiques and jewellery in an historic building.

Plaza 18 de Julio (tel: 84 55 02). Closed Saturday.

Galería Yaiza, Yaiza

Paintings and sculpture, pottery and unusual postcards.

Teguise Market, Lanzarote

Carretera General a Playa Blanca (tel: 83 01 99). Open Monday to Saturday 5–7pm.

TENERIFE
Centro de Artesanía El Limonero, Garachico

Charming courtyard where potters, weavers, instrument-makers and others demonstrate their skills.

Avenida Marítima (opposite Castillo de San Miguel). No telephone.

Salon Canario del Vino, Icod de los Vinos

Excellent range of Canarian wines, both local and from other islands, plus cheese, pastries and liquors. Free tastings.

Plaza de la Pilar, 5.

La Casa de los Balcones, La Orotava

Spectacular historic building with large range of craft and souvenir items - embroidery a speciality.

Calle de San Francisco (tel: 38 28 55). Closed Saturday afternoon.

Casa Iriarte, Puerto de la Cruz

Embroidered tableware and souvenirs in an historic setting.

Calle Iriarte (tel: 38 33 11). Open all day.

Entertainment

*Y*ou're never short on quantity of entertainment in the larger resort areas, but quality and variety is invariably disappointing. It is often a choice between uninspired international cabaret shows and grotesque home-from-home 'fun pubs'. If you want something more, and you are looking for something that is locally inspired, you will have a long search. Smaller resorts are more conducive to the sorts of bars and restaurants where a Spanish guitarist may strike up, but even these are few and far between.

The free magazines *Tenerife Holiday Gazette* and *Lanzarote Holiday Gazette* make entertainment suggestions, but the tourist office is your only guide on Gran Canaria. If you're staying on the other islands, what limited nightlife there is usually revolves around the larger hotels.

CASINOS

Each of the three important tourist islands has at least one casino. The

grandest and oldest is the Casino Taoro, perched high in its own landscaped grounds above Puerto de la Cruz on Tenerife (tel: 38 05 50). It's the sort of place where you might expect to meet James Bond. The casino in Playa de las Américas may not be quite so grand, but it is owned by the same organisation and is thoroughly professional (tel: 79 37 12).

Gran Canaria also has a casino in an impressive setting: the Las Palmas Casino in the Santa Catalina Hotel in Doramas Parque (tel: 24 30 40). The Casino Gran Canaria in the Hotel Meliá Tamarindos in San Agustín (tel: 76 27 24) and the Oasis Gran Casino in the Hotel Oasis, Costa Teguise (Lanzarote, tel: 59 25 25) both reside in plush, modern hotels.

French and American roulette, blackjack and craps are the most common games. The rules are explained nightly before each session (from around 8pm–5am), though that probably won't stop you losing your money. Here are two common-sense rules to cut your losses: decide on your limit in advance and stick to it rigidly; leave your credit cards at the hotel. Once you're out of notes, slot machines will happily gobble up your loose change.

The resort of Playa de Las Américas (Tenerife), one of the main nightlife zones in the islands

Playa de Las Américas presents a mesmerizing show of nightclub neon

You will need your passport and you must be dressed smartly (though not necessarily in jacket and tie) to be allowed admission.

DISCOTHEQUES

The epicentres of the islands' pulsating 18–30 nightlife are Playa de las Américas (Tenerife) and Playa del Inglés (Gran Canaria). Both of these are hectic and the Verónicas area of Playa de las Américas is notorious for attracting more than its fair share of trouble.

Elsewhere, Puerto de la Cruz (Tenerife), Puerto Rico (Gran Canaria) and Puerto del Carmen (Lanzarote) provide the best choice of *discotecas*.

If there is an admission charge then it will normally cover the first drink. Most stay open until 3am, but some go on much later.

The following establishments are among the best of the current crop and have been popular for some little while.

GRAN CANARIA
Dino's, Las Palmas
Los Bardinos Hotel, Calle Eduardo Benot.

San Agustín Beach Club, San Agustín
Playa de los Cocoteros.

LANZAROTE
Joker, Puerto del Carmen
Avenida de las Playas.

TENERIFE
Bugatti's, Playa de las Américas
Opposite Mediterranean Palace Hotel in Tenerife Royal Gardens.

El Coto Up & Down, Puerto de la Cruz
Oro Negro Hotel, Avenida de Colón.

Victoria, Puerto de la Cruz
Avenida de Colón.

CARNAVAL

Carnaval (Carnival) is the biggest, costliest, most frenzied and eagerly awaited event on the islands each year. As soon as one *Carnaval* is finished preparations begin for next year's extravaganza. It takes months to make some of the costumes and the floats are often works of art. More than any other gesture, the huge sums of money spent on *Carnaval* by a people who are so relatively poor demonstrate their love of the fiesta.

Carnaval goes on for two hedonistic weeks with a programme of nightly outdoor dancing, usually to the hottest Latin American dance bands, fancy dress and drag competitions. Stalls selling *cubata* (rum and cola), *churros* (a type of Spanish doughnut) and *pinchitos* (kebabs) are everywhere.

The highlight of all this activity is, of course, the main procession. Comparison with the famous Rio Carnival is obvious, and perhaps not surprising, given

Colourful costumes compete for attention (and prizes) at the Puerto de la Cruz Carnival

the number of Canarios who have emigrated to South America. Drummers beat out pulsating Latin rhythms, while the Carnival Queens stand proud on top of the procession floats in their magnificent dresses and feathered headdresses. The troupes alongside the floats, also dressed to kill, in glitter, feathers and often little else, rumba and samba along the procession route with the vitality and stamina of world-class athletes. Alongside them are drag queens, Charlie Chaplin and Fidel Castro look-alikes plus a multitude of fancy-dressed children.

You will probably see many strange sights during *Carnaval* but none so strange as the final ceremony, known as the Burial of the Sardine. An 8 to 10m-long cardboard/papier-mâché

sardine is dragged to the harbour or the main square accompanied by mourners, invariably men dressed in black drag, theatrically 'weeping' and 'wailing' for all they are worth. At the appointed spot, fireworks inside the sardine are set off and it literally blows itself apart. A grand firework display is then given.

The best places to catch *Carnaval* are Santa Cruz and Puerto de la Cruz on Tenerife, and Las Palmas, Gran Canaria. Dates vary. It starts first in Santa Cruz, ending on Ash Wednesday, then fans out to all other points and other islands. Enquire at the tourist office in advance.

SHOWS

The only common denominator between the following *espectáculos* ('show-spectaculars') is a no-frills, robust attitude to tourist family entertainment. Some of the most popular shows are on tour operators' programmes and the price to the individual is the same as the price for booking through an operator.

GRAN CANARIA
Sioux City

A wild west barbecue and saloon show. *Cañón del Aguila, San Agustín, Gran Canaria (tel: 76 25 73)*.

TENERIFE
Castillo San Miguel

A night of medieval-style jousting is combined (rather incongruously) with the crooning of the 1960s pop stars, the Drifters.
San Miguel Aldea Blanca, 15km east of Playa de las Américas (tel: 70 02 76).

Fiesta Canaria Carnaval

The next best thing to the real *Carnaval* (see pages 146–7) plus Canarian folklore. *Calle Las Toscas, Santa Catalina, Tacoronte (no telephone). Refer to travel agents*.

FLAMENCO

Though it has nothing to do with the Canaries, flamenco shows are regularly staged by the top hotels, and a good flamenco troupe is always worth seeing. Look too for advertisements in bars and restaurants.

The Montaña Tropical centre, Calle Toscon, Puerto del Carmen, Lanzarote (tel: 51 00 23), hosts regular flamenco shows and a *tablao flamenco* (a flamenco floorshow) is also staged at Parque Las Américas at Playa de las Américas, Tenerife.

FOLKLORE

Canarian folklore shows are gentle but enjoyable family affairs with large groups of musicians accompanying a dance troupe in traditional costume. The rhythms are generally Spanish, though lacking the passion of the flamenco, and are played on guitars, flutes and a small ukulele-like instrument called a *timple*.

The best shows are staged in the *Pueblo Canarios* (Canarian Villages) on Gran Canaria (Doramas Parque, Las Palmas, Thursday 5.45pm and Sunday 11.30am, tel: 24 51 35) and Tenerife (Playa de las Américas, Sunday morning). Also worth catching is the Sunday 11 o'clock show at the Hotel Tigaiga, Puerto de la Cruz, Tenerife (tel: 38 35 00), which includes a demonstration of *lucha canaria* (Canarian wrestling).

The famous Lanzarote attraction, Jameos del Agua (see pages 70–1) hosts a popular folklore evening every Tuesday and Saturday night (tel: 83 50 10).

NIGHTCLUBS

A nightclub is distinguished from a mere discotheque by some element of live entertainment and usually also provides a full meal. The following are among the best and also feature on most tour operator group excursions.

GRAN CANARIA
Son a Mar (formerly Scala), San Agustín

Probably the biggest and best known show on the islands, featuring an international cabaret.
Hotel Meliá Tamarindos (tel: 76 68 28).

TENERIFE
Andrómeda, Puerto de la Cruz

Long-legged beauties cavort with

feathers while flamenco dancers remind you that this is Spanish territory.
Lido Martiánez, Avenida de Colón (tel: 38 38 52).

La Cueva, Puerto de la Cruz

An African dance troupe performs African and Hawaiian sets in an old Guanche cave.
Los Realejos, 4km west of Puerto de la Cruz (tel: 34 08 05).

PERFORMING ARTS

The islands are not renowned for their highbrow entertainment and outside the provincial capitals there is very little in the classical sphere.

Opera and classical music, featuring the Orquesta Sinfónica de Tenerife (Tenerife Symphony Orchestra), may be enjoyed at the Teatro Guimerá, Plaza Isla de la Madera, in Santa Cruz (tickets from Cabildo Insular, Santa Cruz, tel: 60 58 01). The performing arts are also well represented in La Laguna and La Orotava but venues here are not advertised to tourists – look in the local papers for details.

In Las Palmas the major classical venue is the Teatro Pérez Galdós (Calle Lentini 1, tel: 36 15 09). The season is from September to May, though special festivals may take place in high summer.

On Gran Canaria classical guitar performances and recitals are given at the Insular Tourism Center, Avenida España, Playa del Inglés (tel: 76 78 48). Pick up a leaflet here to find out what other music and dance events are being staged around the island.

Jazz festivals are held in Puerto de Mogán, Gran Canaria, in March and in La Laguna, Tenerife (enquire about dates).

Sunday morning is the time to enjoy traditionally dressed folk dancers and musicians

Fiestas

*C*anarians love to let their hair down. In fact, to the visitor it sometimes seems that island life is just one big round of parties – religious holidays, island patron saint days, village saint days, city foundation days, a day to celebrate the repulse of an English pirate attack, a day to mark the miraculous discovery of an image of the Virgin, and so on. Add to this the largest annual jamboree, the two-week *Carnaval*, and it's a fair bet that some time during your holiday you will bump into at least one fiesta.

Celebrations typically include a procession, which is secular (marching bands and fancy costumes) or religious, depending upon the event. Sometimes it is a combination of both. The streets come alive with musicians and food and drink vendors, and folk dancing and sometimes Canarian wrestling are staged. Fireworks often round off a fiesta and revelries continue well into the small hours.

There are literally dozens of fiestas throughout the islands. Ask at the tourist office about local events during your

Scenes of pastoral tranquillity decorate a waggon during the Romería de Tegueste

stay. Below are listed the most popular events.

If you're not the sociable type or you value your sleep then you may want to avoid certain places during *Carnaval* and the four- to five-yearly *Bajada* celebrations. Other fiestas should not disturb you unduly.

February
Carnaval (Carnival). The big one (see pages 146–7).

March–April
Semana Santa (Holy Week). Hooded penitents progress through the streets.

June
Corpus Christi. This eight-day religious fiesta is the most important after Carnaval. The highlight is the 'flower carpets', made in many towns and villages. These are huge, colourful pavement artworks (mostly floral or geometric, but sometimes in the form of an Old Master), made of flower petals, coloured sand or salt.

La Orotava and La Laguna, on Tenerife, and Las Palmas, on Gran Canaria are famous for their Corpus Christi carpets. These beautiful works of art are trampled underfoot by the devout during the procession.

If you are not on the islands during

A procession follows a statue of the Virgin during the Romería de Tegueste, Tenerife

Corpus Christi, you may still be able to see a demonstration of 'sand-painting' at Casas de Los Balcones, La Orotava on Tenerife (see page 86).

June/July
Romerías. A *romería* (pilgrimage) can be one of the most colourful celebrations, particularly when the statue of the local Virgin is paraded through the streets on a highly decorated cart pulled by two dressed-up bullocks. There are two very good *romerías* on Tenerife: San Isidro at La Orotava in June, and San Benito Abad at La Laguna on the first Sunday in July.

August
Bajada de la Rama (Descent of the Branch). This popular and joyful fiesta, held on 4 August at Agaete, Gran Canaria, is derived from an ancient Guanche rain-making ritual.

BAJADAS
Aside from the *Bajada de la Rama* at Agaete, there are two other very important *bajadas* ('descents'). On La Palma, the Virgen de las Nieves (Virgin of the Snows) is brought down from her hermitage on 5 August once every five years to the island capital of Santa Cruz. A month of lively celebrations ensues. The next descent is in the year 2,000.

On El Hierro the Virgen de los Reyes (Virgin of the Kings) descends from her forest sanctuary to Valverde on the first weekend in July, once every four years. Her next journey is in 1997.

Accommodation on both islands, scarce at the best of the times, is much sought after during these periods.

Children

*A*ny one of the three major islands can provide an ideal family holiday. In terms of children's activities, Tenerife comes top, followed by Gran Canaria, then Lanzarote. The southern resorts are the best choice on Tenerife and Gran Canaria. Fuerteventura is only recommended if you can make the beach last all day, while the other islands are not geared for children.

The Canarians, like the Spanish, love children and you will rarely have any trouble taking even small children into restaurants or café-bars.

GO-KARTING
Children as young as five can enjoy go-karting while older kids and parents have their own karts and tracks too (see Sport).

NIGHTLIFE
On Tenerife, Castillo San Miguel provides medieval jousting, while on Gran Canaria, Sioux City (good for kids by day too) takes you back to the Wild West. Folklore and flamenco shows are usually never too far away (see pages Entertainment).

'SAFARIS'
Choose your mount from camel, donkey or horse. Camel rides are popular: on Lanzarote in the Montañas del Fuego (see pages 68–9); on Tenerife at El Tanque, near Garachico and at Guaza-Arona; on Gran Canaria at Fataga and Maspalomas (see pages 38–41) and on Fuerteventure at Lajita.

Burros (donkeys) will transport you through the picturesque Barranco de Guayadeque on Gran Canaria (see page 30). Book through a travel agent. Donkey safaris are also available on Tenerife from El Tanque (see above) and from Arafo (tel: 50 04 11). See page 135 for horse-riding.

Whale and dolphin safaris on Tenerife (see pages 134–5) may well appeal to older children.

WATERPARKS
None of the three Canarian waterparks is in the Florida-style big league, but both Aguapark Octopus (Playa de las

Agua Park, Playa de las Américas (Tenerife)

Américas, Tenerife, tel: 79 22 66) and
Ocean Park (just outside Maspalomas,
Gran Canaria, tel: 76 43 61) are
deservedly popular with families.
Aguapark Lanza at Costa Teguise (tel:
51 22 10, open Easter–September) serves
Lanzarote. (*All open daily from around
10am until 5 or 6pm.*)

WATERSPORTS

If your water babies are old enough to
windsurf, you may well be able to find
tuition and small boards at one of the
many schools on the islands (see pages
Sport). Otherwise 'water bananas' and
'ringos' (inflatables pulled behind a
speedboat) splash along at Puerto Rico
(Gran Canaria) and Playa de las
Américas (Tenerife). Pedaloes are also
available here and at Puerto del Carmen
(Lanzarote).

WILDLIFE

Tenerife has four bird and wildlife parks.
By far the biggest and best is the Florida-
style Loro Parque, at Puerto de la Cruz
(see pages 94–5). Other island options

Riding a dromedary on Fuerteventura

are Amazonia and Tenerife Zoo and
Monkey Park (both in the south, see
page 99).

Palmitos Parque is an excellent bird
(and butterfly) park on Gran Canaria
(see page 41) and Guinate Tropical Bird
Park on Lanzarote is also worth a flying
visit (see page 70).

MORE KIDS' STUFF

Cable-car to the top of Mount Teide
(see pages 88–9).
Go wild during *Carnaval* (see pages
146–7).
Tunnel into the magical Cueva (cave)
de los Verdes on Lanzarote (see
page 70).
Have fun at the Maspalomas Holiday
World fair (see page 39).
Visit Montaña Tropical commercial
centre, Puerto del Carmen on
Lanzarote. Tropical birds, remote-
controlled boats, children's shows
(Saturday 11.30am) and flamenco

classes (Saturday 12.30 pm). Catch a
free bus from Avenida de las Playas
(tel: 51 05 82 or 51 00 23.
Ride a horse or a bike (see pages
135 and 137–8).
Dive with the Yellow Submarine (see
pages 134–5). But Parents – note the
prices!
Parents on Tenerife should look out
for the the excellent *Totally Curious
Children's Guide, Tenerife Explored
and Explained*. Try book shops or the
Cabildo Insular office at Plaza de
España, Santa Cruz, for a copy.

ARCHITECTURE

The first Canarians, the Guanches, had little regard for architectural niceties, using the nearest hole in the wall as a home. Caves at least have the benefit of being cool in summer and warm in winter. Not all Guanches lived in caves, however, and it is quite likely that the first Guanche houses were not unlike the small white, one-storey dwellings found in the Canarian countryside today. These *pueblo*-style houses are built of wood, rough rubblework stone, sand and mud. Lanzarote provides the finest examples, trimmed and painted green, their chimneys topped with Moorish-style onion domes.

The Spanish brought Colonial-style architecture to the islands and it still survives in many forms in the older towns of the archipelago. Chief among these is La Laguna, on Tenerife, whose old quarter is a showcase of Spanish-Canarian architecture from the 16th and 17th centuries. Sturdy stone mansions with carved coats of arms and beautifully crafted wooden balconies are the exterior hallmarks of a wealthy merchant's or colonist's home.

The Canaries are famous for their balconies and many modern buildings try to turn the clock back with handcrafted appendages. The wood comes from the heart of the Canarian pine tree and is known as *tea*.

Peer inside the entrance of many an old house and you will find a Moorish-style patio, rich with greenery, perhaps even a fountain and, around the interior, more balconies. The epitome of this style is the Casas de los Balcones in La Orotava, on Tenerife. Elsewhere on Tenerife keep your eyes open in Santa Cruz, Puerto de la Cruz and Garachico, and do pay a visit to the Casa de la Carta museum, near Valle de Guerre, and the History Museum in La Laguna. The La Vegueta district of Las Palmas and the provincial town of Teror are the pride of Gran Canaria, and Teguise on Lanzarote and Santa Cruz de la Palma also feature notable vernacular domestic architecture.

Church architecture on the islands reflects Spanish also colonial style, with two splendid examples of *mudéjar* (Moorish-influenced) ceilings in the principal churches of Santa Cruz de La Palma and La Laguna.

Building sights (clockwise from top to left): Puerto de la Cruz and Taborno (Tenerife), Fataga (Gran Canaria), Betancuria (Fuerteventura), Santa Cruz (Tenerife)

Sport

*T*he clear, warm waters of the islands and the balmy winter climate ensure that the Canaries are a favourite year-round venue for amateur and professional sporting types.

The windy conditions are a plus factor to experienced boardsailers, and Fuerteventura and Tenerife are two of the world's favourite windsurfing destinations. But there are plenty of sheltered bays too, where with a little tuition, beginners can stand upright on a board or on water-skis. The principal watersports centre is Puerto Rico on Gran Canaria, but the south of Tenerife, Fuerteventura and Lanzarote also have much to offer. There are few sporting facilities (on or off the water) on the smaller islands.

Sporting opportunities on dry land are generally not so well developed but golfers will not be disappointed by the quality of courses.

WATERSPORTS

DEEP SEA FISHING

Shark, barracuda, swordfish, sailfish, marlin, tuna and even stingray are all on the big-game menu for the fishermen who charter craft from the many marinas on the islands. The most productive fishing grounds are off the south coast of Gran Canaria, where over 30 world records have been claimed for various types of fish.

If you want to check out the most successful boats, find out what time they return to the marina and see the fishermen pose alongside their catch for the photo-album picture.

The principal charter marinas are: Gran Canaria – Las Palmas (Santa Catalina pier), Pasito Blanco, Puerto Rico; Fuerteventura – Caleta de Fustes/El Castillo; Lanzarote – Playa Blanca; Tenerife – Los Cristianos, Puerto Colón (Playa de la Américas)

DIVING

Diving is very popular in the Canary Islands because of its warm, clear waters. Marine life, wrecks and reefs are not as prolific here as in other more exotic diving destinations in the world, but underwaters parks have been designated at Arinaga, off the east coast of Gran Canaria, and off both the north and south coasts of Fuerteventura.

All the following clubs give tuition.

El Hierro
Restinga
Restinga Dive-In Club

Fuerteventura
Caleta de Fustes/El Castillo
El Castillo Dive Center, *Muelle Deportivo (tel: 87 81 00)*.

Corralejo
Miquel Aballa Dive Center, *Muelle de Corralejo (tel: 86 62 43)*.
The **Trés Islas Hotel** (*tel: 53 57 00*) and **Oliva Beach Hotel** (*tel: 86 61 00*) both organise diving in the designated marine park between Corralejo and Isla de los Lobos.

Jandía
Aldiana Diving Club, *Carretera de*

Jandía (tel: 54 14 47).
Felix (Barakuda) Club. Reef dives twice daily (for experienced divers).
Tel: 54 14 17.
Sotavento Beach Club, *Urbanización Cañada del Río, Costa Calma (tel: 54 70 60).*

Morro del Jable
Los Sargos Diving Club, *Campo de Lucha.*

Gran Canaria
Maspalomas
Náutico School, *Faro Hotel (tel: 14 22 14).*

Playa del Inglés
Sun Sub School, *Buenaventura Beach Hotel (tel: 76 16 50).*

Puerto de Mogán
Top Diving (*tel: 56 56 77).*

Lanzarote
Costa Teguise
NAUI España Diving Associación.

Dive expeditions and wreck diving. *Playa de las Cucharas.*

Puerto del Carmen
Safari Diving. One-day diving safaris plus wreck diving (*tel: 51 14 22).*

Tenerife
Adeje
Club Barracuda, *Hotel Paraíso Floral (tel: 78 07 25).*

Las Galletas
Coralsub–Ten Bel, *TenBel Hotel Complex (tel: 78 52 31/73 00 60).*

Playa de las Américas
Park Club Europe Tenerife (*tel: 75 27 08).*

The Tenerife association (for diving, surfing and windsurfing) is the Centro Insular de Deportes (*tel: 60 56 05 or 24 09 45).*

The coastline of Tenerife provides a magnificent backdrop for paragliding enthusiasts

SAILING

Boats of various sizes can be hired from several sports marinas (*puerto deportivo*) around the islands. Below are some of the principal marinas, local sailing clubs and federations.

Fuerteventura
Jandía
Aldiana Yacht Club. Hobie Cat sailing, *Carretera de Jandía (tel: 54 11 47/48)*.

Gran Canaria
Bahía Felíz
Mistral Club, *Tarajalillo Beach*.
Las Palmas
Federación de Vela (Sailing Federation) *(tel: 29 15 67)*.
Puerto Deportivo (marina office), *Calle Léon y Castillo (tel: 24 41 01)*.
Real Club Náutico de Gran Canaria, *Puerto de la Luz (tel: 23 45 66)*.
Victoria Club, *Paseo de Las Canteras (tel: 26 05 65)*.
Maspalomas
Catamaran Club *(tel: 64 26 31)*.
Maspalomas Yacht Club (Pasito Blanco) *(tel: 76 76 83)*.
Puerto de Mogán
Marina office *(tel: 56 56 68)*.

Puerto Rico
Aristocat, *Puerto Escala (tel: 64 42 91/15 00 10)*.
Escuela Territorial de Vela de Puerto Rico, *Avenida Doreste y Molina (tel: 56 07 72)*.

Lanzarote
Puerto Calero
Marina office *(tel: 51 08 50)*.

Tenerife
Los Cristianos
Puerto Pesquero Los Cristianos, Junta del Puerto (marina office) *(tel: 79 11 02)*.
Los Gigantes
Puerto Deportivo Los Gigantes, Oficina del Puerto (marina office) *(tel: 10 16 01)*.
Playa de las Américas
Puerto Deportivo Colón (marina office) *(tel: 79 36 61/79 45 11)*.
Santa Cruz
Real Club Náutico de Tenerife, *Avenida de Anaga (tel: 27 37 00)*.

SURFING

There is very little organised surfing in the Canaries. It's normally the preserve of the locals who often brave quite dangerous seas and currents. Be careful and never surf alone.

The best locations include: Gran Canaria – Maspalomas Beach and Puerto Rico; Fuerteventura – Isla de los Lobos; Lanzarote – Playa Famara and Playa Martiánez (Puerto de la Cruz).

WATERSKIING

All the following locations offer waterskiing, jet ski-ing and some also do parascending.

Skimming the waves on Tenerife

Fuerteventura
Corralejo Beach.

Gran Canaria
Puerto Rico waterski school
(tel: 56 16 20).

Lanzarote
Costa Teguise
Lanzarote Surf Company, *Playa Las Cucharas (tel: 59 19 74).*
Playa Blanca
Los Delfines Watersports, *Playa Dorada, next to Hotel Playa Dorada.*
Puerto del Carmen
Fariones Beach.

Tenerife
Playa de Las Américas.

WINDSURFING
This sport is so popular throughout the islands that it is practised off almost any reasonable beach. The following are only the main centres, where tuition is usually available. See also pages 58–9.

Fuerteventura
Caleta de Fustes/El Castillo
Fanatic Surf Center *(tel: 86 64 86).*
Corralejo
Ventura Surf *(tel: 86 62 95).*
Fanatic Fun Center, *Hotel Trés Islas (tel: 53 57 00).*
Costa Calma
Fanatic Fun Center, *Playa de Costa Calma, Hotel Monica beach (tel: 86 64 80).*
Jandía
F2 Pro Center, *Los Gorriones Hotel, Playa Barca (tel: 54 70 25).*
Robinson Club, *Playa de Matorral (tel: 54 13 75).*
Bahía Sports, *Commercial Playa Paradiso (tel: 54 02 73).*
Aldiana Yacht Club (see **Sailing**).

Sea, surf and sun, resources that the Canary Islands yield in abundance

Gran Canaria
Las Palmas
Playa de las Canteras.
Maspalomas
Dunkerbeck F2 Windsurfing School
(tel: 76 20 22); **Passat School,** *Aguila Beach* (also beach schools at Playa del Inglés, Bahía Felíz and Las Burras).
Puerto Rico
Sailing School, *Puerto Escala (tel: 56 07 72).*

Lanzarote
Costa Teguise
Lanzarote Surf Company, *Playa Las Cucharas (tel: 59 19 74)*; **International Windsurfing Centre,** *Playa Las Cucharas*
Playa Blanca
Playa Dorada
Puerto del Carmen
Los Fariones, Playa de los Pocillos, Matagorda and Las Gaviotas.

Tenerife
El Médano
Sunwind, *Avenida Islas Canarias (tel: 17 61 74).*
Playa de las Américas.
Opposite Palm Beach Club.

LAND SPORTS – PARTICIPATORY

CYCLING
Mountain bikes are widely available for hire from major resorts on Gran Canaria, Fuerteventura, Lanzarote and Tenerife.

GOLF
There is still only a handful of clubs on the islands, but quality is good. All the following have a driving range, practice putting green, club and trolley hire and club house.

Gran Canaria
Campo de Golf Maspalomas
Beautiful location on the edge of the dunes and the oasis. 18 holes, 6,216m.
Avenida TO Neckermann (tel: 76 25 81).
Real Club de Golf de Las Palmas (Club Bandama)
This century-old club was the first ever to be formed on Spanish territory and enjoys a quite magnificent setting on the edge of the Caldera de Bandama. 18 holes, 5,679m.
Santa Brígida, 14km southwest of Las Palmas (tel: 35 10 50).

Lanzarote
Club de Golf de Costa Teguise
Handicap required: 28 men, 36 women. 18 holes.
Avenida de Golf, Costa Teguise (tel: 59 05 12).

Tenerife
Golf Club Amarilla
18 holes.
Amarilla Country Club, San Miguel de Abona (tel: 79 24 61/79 35 59/78 57 77).
Golf del Sur
Home to the Tenerife Open. Handicap necessary. 27 holes.
San Miguel de Abona, Autopista del Sur, km 61, 5 (tel: 70 45 55).
Golf Tenerife El Peñón
18 holes, 5,200m.
Tacoronte (tel: 25 02 40/25 02 30).

Club Bandama – Spain's oldest golf course

A new course is currently under construction near Puerto del Carmen, Lanzarote.

GO-KARTING
Tracks vary in speed, size and facilities. All have karts that range from child-sized to adult-sized.

Gran Canaria
Gran Karting Club
Claimed to be the largest track in the world at 1,650m; also features mini-motor bikes for children aged over 10. *Carretera General del Sur, km 46, Tarajalillo, Maspalomas (tel: 76 00 90)*.

Lanzarote
Eurokart, *San Bartolomé (tel: 59 00 28)*.

Tenerife
Karting Club Tenerife, *Carretera de Cho, km 66 Guaza, Las Chafiras, Arona (tel: 78 66 20)*.
Karting Club Las Américas, *Carretera General del Sur, Adeje (tel: 71 00 96/78 05 84)*.

TENNIS
Two of the best tennis centres on the islands are on Tenerife. Tournaments are held every Wednesday in Playa de las Américas at the Hotel Las Palmeras, where tuition and floodlit courts are available *(tel: 79 09 91)*. The TenBel Hotel complex has similar facilities *(tel: 73 00 60)*. Serious players should also consider Club La Santa, near Tinajo, on the east coast of Lanzarote *(tel: 84 01 01)*.

SPECTATOR SPORTS

FOOTBALL
CD Tenerife, whose home ground is in Santa Cruz, plays in the Spanish 1st Division and hosts the likes of Barcelona

> **JUMP TO IT!**
> *Parapente* (para-gliding) is a relatively new Canary Island sport, similar to hang-gliding, but using a parachute-like wing. If you would like to fling yourself off a Tenerife hillside and man your own flight, contact one of the following clubs: Aeroclub Maspalomas (*tel: 76 24 47*); Paraclub Teide, Avenida Santa Cruz 29 (no tel: number; Club Parapente Alisios (*tel: 20 03 51*); Parapente Club del Sur (*tel: 78 13 57*); Parapente Tenerife (*tel: 52 42 63*). The Aeroclub Maspalomas runs three-day beginners' parachute courses, culminating in a jump onto the dunes.

and Real Madrid. Matches are usually on a Saturday evening or a Sunday. See the local papers for details.

On Gran Canaria a mini-international tournament is held in January at Maspalomas. This comprises four top teams from Germany, Norway, Holland and Sweden.

SAILING (*Vela Lateena*)
On Gran Canaria, traditional Canarian sailing *lateens* (small crafts with large triangular sails) race off Las Palmas and Puerto Rico on Saturday afternoons and Sunday mornings between April and September.

WRESTLING (*Lucha Canaria*)
This traditional fighting sport is likely to appeal to fans of Sumo wrestling. The basic objective is to throw your opponent to the ground, but there are other rituals to be observed. The sport is active on all the islands and most villages have a team comprising 12 wrestlers.

Food and Drink

*C*anarian food is tasty, fresh and filling, though rarely glamorous. Unfortunately, on the larger islands, it's usually easier to find a 'Real British Pub' or a fast-food restaurant than a Canarian *tipico* (typical native restaurant). The latter is distinguished by a relatively short menu of soups, stews and grilled fish dishes. If you can't find a *tipico*, the best alternative for local food is a place serving *tapas*. This is the Spanish custom of serving small portions of local food in informal restaurant or bar surroundings. *Tapas* bars, however, are also quite thin on the ground in the tourist centres.

Canarian cuisine

Canarian cuisine is essentially peasant and fishermen's food. Meat only usually features as part of a stew (usually pork, veal or rabbit) and steaks, generally imported from Spain or South America, are for tourists only.

Soupy stews are the most typical Canarian meals. *Potaje* has only vegetables; add meat to make *rancho canario* and add more meat still to make *puchero*. This is, of course, a generalisation; each is flavoured differently, with herbs such as thyme, saffron, marjoram, parsley and particularly cumin and coriander, but basic ingredients are similar. A Guanche staple, *gofio* (maize meal), once eaten as bread, is still used to thicken stews. Another common stew is *garbanzo compuesto* (chick-pea stew with meat), often available as a *tapas*.

Perfect partners – local red wine and goat's cheese!

The waters of the southern Atlantic are a rich breeding ground for many species of fish

Other typical Canarian casserole dishes are *sancocho*, a stew of salted fish (often seabass) and *conejo con salmorejo* (rabbit in a spicy, tomato-based sauce).

Fresh fish is always on the menu and seaside restaurants can offer a bewildering and untranslatable fish list (although it's rarely the case that everything listed on the menu is available). The method of cooking is usually plain – either boiled, fried or grilled (often on a barbecue). As an accompaniment you will be served salad and *papas arrugadas* ('wrinkled potatoes'). The latter are small potatoes, boiled in their jackets in very salty water. On the table there will be two cold olive oil-based sauces; red *mojo picón* ('piquant sauce') and *mojo verde* ('green sauce'). The latter is a cool parsley and coriander sauce, perfect with fish; the former is a spicy chilli and paprika mix, generally poured over potatoes and/or red meat.

The most famous Canarian dessert is *bienmesabe*, a concoction of honey, almonds and rum. Despite its frequent appearance on menus, it is rarely available, and you may have to make do with the ubiquitous Spanish *flan* (a cooked milk dessert, like creme-caramel)

Do try the local cheese, wherever you are. This is always made from goat's milk and is invariably good.

Drinks

Lanzarote and La Palma are famous for their malvasia-style wines, grown on the volcanic soil. These come in dry, as well as sweet styles and are generally good quality, the best being rich and full bodied.

Canarian after-dinner drinks include *mistel* (a sweet wine) and *parra* (a firewater-style *aguardiente* brandy) though these are not common. *Ronmiel* ('rum-honey') is to be found everywhere. White cane-spirit rum is made on Gran Canaria; the 'honey' is actually sap from the palm tree, gathered in La Gomera. The resultant cocktail is a pleasant, smooth, orange-tasting drink, resembling neither conventional rum nor honey!

CAFÉ LIFE

If you want to see real Canarians at play, just walk into any busy café, buy a coffee or a beer and take a ringside seat. Cafés are usually fairly spartan, noisy recreational meeting areas, male-oriented (though women do go there, too) and tolerant of children any time of day or night.

Spain is (officially) one of the noisiest places in the world and many Canarian cafés seem to take it upon themselves to uphold this tradition. The television can be on from the day's first children's cartoon, through the dreadful afternoon soap operas, to the evening game shows. Hardly anyone is watching and most probably cannot hear what is going on anyway, for the radio behind the bar, or the fruit machine in the corner, filling the whole café with loud electronic tones. No wonder the locals shout and gesticulate at each other – it's the only way to be heard!

The only time the TV really draws the audience is when a football match is on. CD Tenerife are the local favourites;

otherwise the crowd will cheer for Barcelona, or indeed anyone else who will put Real Madrid's nose out of joint.

Locals may add to the cacophony by striking the metal bar with coins to grab the barmen's attention. Alcoholic drinks are served at any time, in devil-may-care measures, though most locals start the day with a *café solo* (black coffee). Tourists generally order *café con leche* (coffee with milk), while those who want an alternative between harsh black and sweet or, milky white opt for a *cortado* (small with a little milk). *Donuts* (it's the same word) and tostada (toast) are usually available for breakfast. After a quick scan of the papers and a word to their friends, those who have work to go to, depart. Those who don't, and the older retired men, sit down for a game of dominoes or cards; and around midday the *tapas* is unveiled.

Eating out

Eating out is relatively inexpensive. In the resorts competition tends to keep prices down (though this may be at the expense of quality), and in the villages eating out is generally priced for the locals. If you don't mind fairly basic amenities and a menu with little choice, and you can manage a few words of Spanish, the latter is nearly always better value and more enjoyable. Portions are usually large and a typical Canarian soup-stew starter may well suffice as a main course.

In the listings of recommended restaurants the approximate cost of a three-course meal per person with a half-bottle of wine, or a couple of beers, is indicated by the following symbols:

★ = 1,250 ptas–1,750 ptas
★★ = 1,750 ptas–2,500 ptas
★★★ = 2,500 ptas–3,500 ptas
★★★★ over 3,500 ptas

EL HIERRO
Mirador de la Peña ★★
Canarian and island specialities are served in tranquil surroundings, with panoramic views.
Guarazoca (tel: 55 03 00).

FUERTEVENTURA
ANTIGUA
El Molino ★★
Fuerteventuran specialities are served in an atmospheric former granary building.
Carretera del Sur, km 19 (tel: 87 82 20).

CORRALEJO
La Marquesina ★★
Locals and tourists mix in this unpretentious harbourside fish restaurant.
Muelle Viejo, old town harbour (tel: 53 54 35).

LAS PLAYITAS
Casa Enrique ★/★★
All kinds of local fish are on offer in this bright friendly, modern quayside establishment.
Calle San Pedro, 26 (tel: 16 20 68).

GRAN CANARIA
CRUZ DE TEJEDA
Parador Nacional ★★★
Excellent and inventive Canarian specialities served in the *parador* dining room (avoid the front terrace).
Cruz de Tejeda (tel: 65 80 50).

LAS PALMAS AND ENVIRONS
El Cerdo Que Rie ★★
Convivial basement restaurant, famous for its Spanish food, fondues and flambés.
Paseo de Las Canteras, 31 (no telephone).
El Novillo Precoz ★★
Hearty portions of barbecued meat South American style are the speciality here.
Calle Portugal, 9, behind Playa de las Canteras (tel: 22 16 59).
Jardín Canario ★★★
High-quality Canarian and international food overlooking the botanic gardens.
Carretera de las Palmas, Tafira Alta (tel: 35 16 45).
La Parilla ★★★★
Superb international cuisine on the 8th floor of this 5-star hotel.
Hotel Reina Isabel, Calle Alfredo L Jones 40 (tel: 26 01 00).

MASPALOMAS
Orangerie ★★★
A creative blend of Canarian, Spanish and international styles.

A typical counter display to tempt the tastebuds

*Palm Beach Hotel, Avenida del Oasis,
Maspalomas (tel: 14 08 06).*

MOGÁN
Acaymo ★★
Excellent rustic restaurant serving
Canarian specialities.
Calle San José, Mogán (tel: 56 92 63).

PLAYA DEL INGLÉS
La Toja ★★★
Small, pleasant restaurant serving
superb Galician dishes.
*Edificio Barbados, Avenida de Tirajana
(tel: 76 11 96).*
Tenderete II ★★
Canarian cuisine with seafood specials
served in simple, attractive
surroundings.
Avenida de Tirajana (tel: 76 14 60).

PUERTO DE LAS NIEVES
Dedo de Dios ★★
Bright, airy fish restaurant with views of
the impressive Dedo de Dios rock stack.
The harbour (tel: 89 80 00).

SAN AGUSTÍN
San Agustín Beach Club ★★★★
Book a table by the pool for the area's
best international and seafood cuisine.
Playa de los Cocoteros (tel: 76 04 00).

LA GOMERA
LAS ROSAS
Las Rosas ★★
Canarian food, wonderful views and a
demonstration of *el silbo* (see page 115);
popular with coach parties. Lunch only.
Carretera General (tel: 80 09 16).

PLAYA DE SANTIAGO
Hotel Tecina ★★★★
Request a balcony table to enjoy
excellent international-Canarian cuisine
with a stupendous view.
Lomada de Tecina (tel: 89 50 50).

SAN SEBÁSTIAN
Conde de La Gomera Parador ★★★★
Superb innovative Canarian dishes in a
very convincing mock-historic setting.
Balcón de la Ville y Puerto (tel: 87 11 00).

LA PALMA
SAN NICOLÁS
Bodegón Tamanca *
Rustic cave bar serving local food in generous helpings.
Las Manchas, 10km south Los Llanos de Aridane (tel: 46 21 55).

SANTA CRUZ AND ENVIRONS
Parilla Chipi Chipi **
Attractive garden restaurant famous for its barbecued fish and meats.
Velhoco, Carretera de Las Nieves (tel: 41 76 00).
Restaurante Canarias *
Functional but friendly modern seafront establishment offering good-value Canarian dishes.
Avenida Marítima (tel: 41 10 00).

LANZAROTE
ARRECIFE
Castillo de San José ***
Elegant, calm, modern restaurant with panoramic seaviews, serving excellent Canarian food.
Carretera Costa Teguise, north of town centre (tel: 81 10 60/81 23 21).

COSTA TEGUISE
La Chimenea ***
Elegant beachside dining from an international menu. Closed Sundays and July.
Playa de las Cucharas (tel: 81 47 00).

HARÍA
Mirador de la Valle **
Small, friendly, *mirador* restaurant serving fresh fish and lamb specials. Closed Tuesday.
Los Valles, km 17.8 (south of Haría).

MONTAÑAS DEL FUEGO
El Diablo **
All cooking is done on the grill above the live volcano. Superb views over the Mountains of Fire.
Islote del Hilario, Parque Nacional de Timanfaya (tel: 84 00 57).

PUERTO DEL CARMEN
El Sardinero **
The town's most famous fish restaurant. Book a first-floor window table to watch the locals playing *boules*.
Plaza El Varadero (tel: 51 19 33).
La Sardina Flamenca **
Good international and local food is served in this modern restaurant. Flamenco dancing is regularly staged for the clientele.
Montaña Tropical, Calle Toscon (tel: 51 00 23).

TEGUISE
Acatife **
Fine Canarian and Spanish specialities are served in a historic setting. Closed Sunday and Monday.
Plaza de la Constitución (tel: 84 50 37).

A simply decorated *tipico* in Playa de Las Américas (Tenerife)

El Méson de Paco ★★/★★★
Local and international food served in
250-year-old house. Closed Tuesday.
Calle Dacil, 6 (tel: 84 56 11).

YAIZA
La Era ★★
This picture-book Canarian *tipico* is
renowned for its Canarian cuisine.
*Signposted off Carretera General
(tel: 83 00 16).*

TENERIFE
CAÑADAS DEL TEIDE
Parador de Cañadas del Teide ★★★
A bright, modern, bustling dining room
serving superb Canarian dishes.
*Parque Nacional del Teide, opposite Los
Roques (tel: 38 64 15).*

GARACHICO
Isla Baja ★★
A popular fish restaurant overlooking the
front, with a model which shows the
18th-century town's destruction.
Calle Esteban de Ponte, 5 (tel. 83 00 08).

ICOD DE LOS VINOS
Carmen ★
Canarian food and *tapas* are on offer in
this charming local-style house. Closed
Wednesday.
Calle Hércules, 2 (tel: 81 06 31).

LOS CRISTIANOS
El Bote ★
This tiny boat-shaped bar serves the best
tapas in Los Cristianos/Playa de las
Américas.
*Calle El Cabezo (behind the harbour
promenade). No telephone.*
El Sol ★★★
Classic French cuisine is prepared by the
owner-chef at this popular restaurant.
The port (tel: 70 05 69).

A *tipico* in the Edificio Rincon del Puerto,
Puerto de la Cruz (Tenerife)

PLAYA DE LAS AMÉRICAS
El Dornajo ★
A *tipico* where good quality and quantity
is supervised by the owner-chef.
Avenida Litoral (tel: 79 14 25).

PUERTO DE LA CRUZ AND
ENVIRONS
El Lagar ★★★
Top quality international cuisine popular
with ex-patriates and locals.
*Santa Úrsula, La Cuesta de la Villa (tel:
30 08 75).*
Magnolia ★★★★
Superb Catalan and international
cuisine.
*Carretera del Botánico, 5, Urbanización La
Paz (tel: 38 56 14).*
Mario ★★/★★★
Small fish restaurant in the pretty Rincón
del Puerto courtyard complex. Closed
Monday.
*Edificio Rincón del Puerto, Plaza El Charco
(tel: 38 55 35).*
Mi Vaca y Yo ★★★
Charming typical Canarian rustic setting
for excellent local and international
cuisine, particularly seafood. Dinner
only.
Calle Cruz Verde, 3 (tel: 38 52 47).

Hotels and Accommodation

*T*he vast majority of tourist accommodation in the Canary Islands has been built over the last 20 years to cater for package holidaymakers. This has been mostly concentrated in the large resorts of southern Tenerife and southern Gran Canaria, but the south of Fuerteventura and Costa Teguise and Puerto del Carmen on Lanzarote have also been built up. The small islands, however, have hardly been touched. There is just one large hotel on both La Gomera and La Palma, and El Hierro is still virtually unknown territory.

Unfortunately for independent travellers, there is no tradition of private accommodation (as, for example, in the Greek Islands) nor the small type of family-run hotels that are found in mainland Spain. Only in the older resorts, the two major island capitals and the odd village here and there, is it possible to find 'unpackaged' accommodation.

Hostales

Hostales, designated by the sign Hs, are of a lower standard than hotels and are graded from 1 to 3 stars. Facilities in a 3-star *hostal* should be the equivalent of a reasonable 2-star hotel, but don't expect much in 1- or 2-star places. There are very few of these establishments (look in Santa Cruz de Tenerife, El Hierro and Arrecife, Lanzarote).

Hotels

Pick up any holiday brochure and you will find page upon page of characterless Canarian hotels, all built to a similar 3- or 4-star standard. These provide comfortable, well-equipped rooms, a swimming pool, bars, possibly a discotheque, live nightly entertainments, sports facilities, 'boutiques' and so on. Many of these are large (around 300 rooms) and high rise, and a good number are still raw around the edges.

Cheap hotels (below a 3-star grading) are thin on the ground. Try Las Palmas, Santa Cruz de Tenerife, Puerto de la Cruz and Fuerteventura.

Travellers putting together their own package in 3- or 4-star hotels (or apartments) are advised to book well ahead and shop around for prices. The hotel's stated nightly rates often bear little resemblance to what may be negotiated. In general, however, it would be difficult to beat the price of a late availability package.

Hotelapartamentos

Hotelapartments, or aparthotels, feature rooms with their own kitchen facilities, yet retain most of the other trappings of an ordinary hotel. These are popular in most large resorts.

Paradores

Paradores are state-run hotels, renowned for providing the best accommodation available in any particular region of Spain. All the Canary Islands once had *paradores*, but the one on Lanzarote (at Arrecife) closed and Gran Canaria's *parador* is now just a restaurant. The other five survivors all succeed in their stated aim of reflecting local style and décor and providing the very best in local and regional cooking.

The days when *paradores* were a

Apartamentos Lanzamar – typical low-rise accommodation on Lanzarote

cheap way of seeing Spain have long gone. They are now classified like other hotels, from 1 to 5 stars, and charge commercial rates.

The best (and most expensive) establishment is the mock-colonial Conde de la Gomera, an attraction in its own right, and recognised as one of the finest small *paradores* in all Spain (see page 111).

The other *paradores* are no less individual. Fuerteventura's modern *parador* at Puerto del Rosario resembles (surely unintentionally) the town's foreign legion barracks, but is really quite comfortable inside; Tenerife's Cañadas del Teide *parador* resembles a mountain chalet, cosy and popular with walkers;

Santa Cruz de la Palma's *parador* merges seamlessly with the traditional seafront houses. If you really want to get away from the crowds, El Hierro's modern-traditional *parador*, set at the end of a road going nowhere on the loneliest island of them all, is the last word in solitude. All, apart from Santa Cruz, have their own swimming pools.

For central bookings contact Paradores de Turismo de España, Requena 3, 28013 Madrid (tel: (01) 559 0069, fax (01) 559 3233). In the UK contact Keytel International, 402 Edgware Road, London W2 1ED (0171 402 8182). Enquire at the Spanish National/Tourist Office in other countries.

Pensiones

A *pensión* (guest house) is a relatively rare sight in the islands. The best place to look is in Puerto de la Cruz, Tenerife, where there is a choice of nine. However, by nature, these are very small and, given Puerto's popularity, the best are likely to be booked in advance. Write to the Puerto tourist office (see page 94) or your own Spanish National Tourist Office for a list of these.

Elsewhere on Tenerife there is a handful of *pensiones* in Santa Cruz and the smaller towns on the island. There is a choice of six on La Palma. The Pension Cubana in Santa Cruz de La Palma is particularly notable for its excellent state of preservation, its antique furnishings and its ideal location.

Las Palmas, Gran Canaria, has several *pensiones* but only hardy travellers should consider staying in the back streets where some of these are located.

The parador in the Teide National Park is a comfortable mountain lodge

Self-catering

Self-catering bungalows and apartments are a popular holiday choice and are usually grouped together in developments known as *urbanizaciónes*. These also often include time-share apartments.

If you would like an apartment away from the tourist ghettos, ask the local tourist office for details (many of these are only for rent for a minimum period of a month) or, before you go, consult one of the smaller specialist island operators.

Camping

Given the ideal climate for camping, sites are surprisingly few and far between. There are only eight official sites on the islands but *camping sauvage* ('wild camping' – off-site) is tolerated in many places. Enquire at the local tourist office to reduce the chance of being moved on by jealous farmers or land-owners.

Tenerife has just one official site: the well-equipped Nauta Camping/Caravanning at Las Galletas on the south coast (tel: 78 51 18). If you do see backpackers on southern Tenerife it is likely they are off to La Gomera – probably to the Valle Gran Rey, which is popular with campers and those in search of an alternative life-style.

There is one designated site on La Gomera, at Caserio de Cedro on the edge of the Garajonay National Park. This is administered by the island government office and if you wish to camp here you should contact the office in San Sebastián de La Gomera, Carretera General del Sur 20 (tel: 87 01 05). Camping within the National Park is strictly forbidden on La Gomera, as it is on Tenerife and Lanzarote. Climbers and keen walkers in the Teide National Park however may apply to use the

The charming, atmospheric Parador Conde de la Gomera

spartan mountain refuge at Altavista (contact ICONA, Santa Cruz, Tenerife, tel: 28 35 58).

La Palma permits camping in the National Park (maximum stay two nights) as long as permission is sought in advance. The site is below Roque Salvaje (1½–2 hours' walk from Los Brecitos). Apply to Parque Nacional de la Caldera de Taburiente, Calle O'Daly, 35, Santa Cruz de la Palma (tel: 41 31 41).

Gran Canaria has four sites. The two official ones are Camping Guantánamo at La Playa de Tauro near Puerto Rico (tel: 56 02 07 or 24 17 01) and Camping Temisas, Lomo de la Cruz, on the road from Agüimes to San Bartolomé de Tirajana (tel: 79 81 49). Both are well equipped, but Temisas can only accommodate 50 people. There are two other (unofficial) sites at Pasito Blanco and Fataga (enquire at the Maspalomas tourist office for more details).

There are no official sites on Fuerteventura, Lanzarote or El Hierro.

Time Share

Time Share is a much maligned accommodation option, largely on account of the unsavoury get-rich-quick characters it seems to attract. There is, however, nothing inherently wrong with the concept and most time-share organisations offer exchange facilities, should you tire of your original choice or should your personal circumstances change.

There are no specific rules that apply to buying time-share packages in the Canaries that don't apply generally anywhere else. The two golden rules to apply are never sign anything while on holiday (get home and 'cool off' first) or without sound legal advice. It would also seem common sense to avoid the overtures of the often loutish street-corner touts.

Youth hostels

There are no Youth Hostels or similar associations on the islands.

On Business

*T*he Canary Islands are no longer the trade hub that their geographical position, half-way between Europe, Africa and the Americas, once made them. Trade routes have changed and ships which once stopped here for refuelling and 'rest and recreation' can now sail by, or they have been replaced with air travel and more fashionable destinations.

The island's only business cities are the provincial capitals of Las Palmas and Santa Cruz de Tenerife. Both rely heavily on oil-refining. Santa Cruz is one of the largest refiners in all Spain, processing Venezuelan crude for domestic use. In terms of international trade and commerce Las Palmas is much more important than Santa Cruz, attracting 8,000 ships a year. Around five million tons of freight (mostly oil and petroleum) flow in, and one million tons of foodstuffs flow out, mostly to Spain.

As part of Spain and therefore a member of the European Union, the islands enforce EU trading conditions. If you require information on any aspect of trading in the Canaries before you depart, write with full details (no telephone requests dealt with) to: The Spanish Commercial Office, 66 Chilterns Street, London W1.

Las Palmas is a bustling commercial city

Business etiquette
Canarians are generally friendly, easy-going people who will often suggest talking business over a slap-up lunch. Don't think this is wasted time or effort. Life is slower here in most aspects than on mainland Europe (though Las Palmas on Gran Canaria is an exception) but don't take this as a sign of provincial naïvety. Many successful businessmen have moved from mainland Spain to the Canaries to facilitate or oversee their import-export trades and have a keen eye for the next business opportunity.

Business services
Tenerife, Gran Canaria and Lanzarote have sizeable ex-patriate communities (mostly English, but also German and Scandinavian), who supply and use business services. Pick up any of the English-language publications (see Media, page 184) and you will find advertisements for office equipment, computer supplies, secretarial, translation and interpretation services, removals and freight, messengers and all manner of insurance, investment and financial brokers.

If you are planning to set up your own business on the islands, or to take any legal or financial advice, be very careful. As one of the advertisements frankly admits, 'it's a minefield!'.

One useful publication might be *You and the Law in Spain*, available from

Lookout Publications SA, Puebla Lucia, 29460 Fuengirola, Málaga, Spain.

Conferences

For 'olde-worlde' style, the *parador* on La Gomera is a perfect venue, with little to distract delegates from serious business. Another choice on the island is the excellent Hotel Tecina. A young sales team might appreciate the amusements of Playa de las Américas on Tenerife. There are several hotels with convention halls in the resort. Chief among these is the luxurious Grand Hotel Mediterranean Palace, one of the very few hotels on the islands that actively promote themselves as convention hotels (it is a member of Expo Grupo, see below). Puerto de la Cruz, in the north of the island, is a good half-way house, with traditional class but plenty of modern amenities too. In Santa Cruz the only hotel with more than a 3-star rating is the beautiful but expensive 5-star Mencey.

Impromptu street business

On Gran Canaria there are several large impressive 4- and 5-star hotels in Las Palmas with conference facilities. The other good place for a serious conference is Maspalomas, with its smart hotels by the oasis.

On Lanzarote, Puerto del Carmen and Playa Blanca are possibilities but the quieter, more up-market Costa Teguise is probably the best bet, particularly if your budget stretches to the Meliá Salinas hotel.

One of the two large hotels on Corralejo beach is the natural choice on Fuerteventura.

The only hotel that a business conference organiser would consider on La Palma is the Sol La Palma at Puerto Naos. If the theme of the conference is getting away from it all, the *parador* on El Hierro is the perfect choice.

All of the venues mentioned above are 4-star standard or above and have a conference hall, but it is unlikely that many of them will be as well equipped with the sound and light facilities that are standard in major world business centres.

Most of the hotels capable of staging conferences belong to groups. Contact them on the following central reservations or head office numbers:

Expo Grupo (Barcelona) tel: 325 81 00.
Hesperia (Barcelona) tel: 218 03 00.
Iberotel (Majorca) tel: 20 00 11.
Ifa (Gran Canaria) tel: 77 00 22.
NH Hoteles (Barcelona) tel: 418 63 22.
Paradores (Madrid) tel: 559 00 69 (UK – Keytel International tel: 0171 402 8182).
Sol/Meliá Hoteles (Majorca) tel: 29 89 66.
Tryp Hoteles (Madrid) tel: 315 32 46.

Practical Guide

CONTENTS

ARRIVING

Visitors from EU countries, North America, Canada, Australia and New Zealand only need a passport to enter the Canary Islands. A visa is necessary if you intend to stay for longer than 90 days.

By air

There are international airports on Gran Canaria (tel: 25 46 40), Fuerteventura (tel: 85 12 50), Lanzarote (tel: 81 03 50) and Tenerife. Tenerife has two international airports; Tenerife North/Los Rodeos (tel: 25 77 45) and Tenerife South/Reina Sofía (tel: 77 00 50), which is the main one. Each of the other islands has an airport for inter-island flights (La Gomera's is under construction).

Regular airport buses go from: Gran Canaria airport to Las Palmas and Maspalomas; from Tenerife North

airport to Puerto de la Cruz; and from Tenerife South to Los Cristianos/Playa de las Américas. There are also express buses which link the two airports. Regular local bus services also run from other island airports. All airports have taxis to meet inter-island flights.

By boat

There are no regular cruise liner services to the Canaries, though cruise ship do sometimes call at Las Palmas and La Gomera. From mainland Spain, ships sail from Cádiz to Santa Cruz de Tenerife, Las Palmas on Gran Canaria and to Arrecife on Lanzarote. Trasmediterránea operate between Cádiz, Tenerife and Gran Canaria (see Ferries, page 187).

CAMPING

Given the scarcity of good, cheap

accommodation on the islands, this is one of the few budget options. However, there are few official campsites, so be prepared to rough it (see pages 172–3).

CHILDREN

The more popular Canary Islands are completely geared for family holidays and within the major resorts you will find all you need in the way of babycare products. Babysitters can be found for older children and many hotels have specific children's activities and 'clubs'.

CLIMATE

For all-year-round sunshine you'll have to go to the south of Gran Canaria or the south of Tenerife. The small westerly islands can be quite cool, though for most of the winter they are pleasantly spring-like to North Europeans.

If you're visiting the north of the larger islands, be prepared for some rain and cooler temperatures in the winter. Winds can also be strong. Summer sunshine is virtually guaranteed everywhere.

CONVERSION CHARTS

See tables opposite

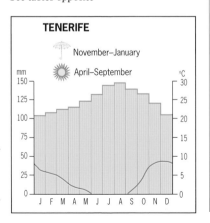

TENERIFE

November–January
April–September

Conversion Table

FROM	TO	MULTIPLY BY
Inches	Centimetres	2.54
Feet	Metres	0.3048
Yards	Metres	0.9144
Miles	Kilometres	1.6090
Acres	Hectares	0.4047
Gallons	Litres	4.5460
Ounces	Grams	28.35
Pounds	Grams	453.6
Pounds	Kilograms	0.4536
Tons	Tonnes	1.0160

To convert back, for example from centimetres to inches, divide by the number in the third column.

Men's Suits

UK		36	38	40	42	44	46	48
Rest of Europe	46	48	50	52	54	56	58
US		36	38	40	42	44	46	48

Dress Sizes

UK		8	10	12	14	16	18
France		36	38	40	42	44	46
Italy		38	40	42	44	46	48
Rest of Europe		34	36	38	40	42	44
US		6	8	10	12	14	16

Men's Shirts

UK	14	14.5		15	15.5	16	16.5	17
Rest of Europe	36	37		38	39/40	41	42	43
US	14	14.5		15	15.5	16	16.5	17

Men's Shoes

UK		7	7.5	8.5		9.5	10.5	11
Rest of Europe	41		42	43		44		45	46
US		8	8.5	9.5		10.5	11.5	12

Women's Shoes

UK		4.5	5	5.5	6		6.5	7
Rest of Europe	38	38	39	39		40	41
US		6	6.5	7	7.5		8	8.5

The Tenerife–La Gomera ferry

CRIME

Theft from cars is the most common form of crime against tourists on the islands. Never leave anything of value in your car, even locked in the boot. If you are parked for any length of time in the streets of Las Palmas you can almost guarantee that your car will be opened. Other Canarian towns and villages are by no means as bad, however, and the epidemic here is not comparable with that on the mainland.

Hotels usually have safes for hire, though staff are invariably very honest and break-ins at good hotels are rare. Apartments are less easy to police, so be on your guard.

Violence against tourists is unusual but don't tempt fate by treading the seamier streets of Las Palmas after dark.

If you are a victim of robbery and wish to make a claim against your insurance policy, report the incident to the local police who will give you a copy of your statement for this purpose.

CUSTOMS REGULATIONS

There are no limits on the amounts of alcohol and tobacco that can be brought onto the islands, but the prices of these products are so low in the Canaries that it seems a pointless exercise.

Despite the Canaries' EU status the restricted export duty-free limits on drinks, tobacco, perfumes etc are still in force: 200 cigarettes or 100 cigarillos or 250g tobacco or 50 cigars; 1 litre of spirits over 22° proof or 2 litres fortified or sparkling wine, plus 2 litres of still wine; 60cc perfume or 250cc toilet water; £32 worth of gifts per person, but not more than 50 litres of beer or 25 cigarette lighters.

DISABLED TRAVELLERS

There are wheelchair facilities at all the international terminals and as hotels and apartments continue to be built, so more choice becomes available for the wheelchair user. In all there are 74 hotels and hotelapartments (HA) on the islands which claim to have wheelchair access and/or facilities. Most of these are in the newer resorts of Playa del Inglés on Gran Canaria (11 hotels) and Playa de las Américas (26 hotels) on Tenerife. The only other resort that can offer a reasonable choice is Puerto de la Cruz, with eight wheelchair-friendly hotels. However even the smaller islands have at least one suitable accommodation each.

There are two purpose-built centres on the islands for the disabled holidaymaker. On Tenerife in Los Cristianos is the Mar y Sol resort. For direct information tel: 79 54 73; for information from the UK contact ATS Travel, 1 Tankhill Road, Purfleet, Essex tel: 01708 863198. On Lanzarote in Puerto del Carmen is Casas Heddy, a Norwegian-inspired enterprise. For details and bookings write to Postboks 3083, Elisenberg 0207, Oslo 2, Norway.

General facilities throughout the islands are poor to non-existent. There are very few adapted toilets, no adapted public transport facilities or adapted hire cars (even automatics are rare). Kerbs are generally high and the terrain is often steep.

The Spanish association for disabled travellers is Federation ECOM, Gran Vía de las Corts Catalanes 562-2a, 08011, Barcelona (tel: 217 38 82). UK travellers should contact the Holiday Care Service for their special fact sheets on Gran Canaria, Lanzarote and Tenerife and for any general advice: 2, Old Bank Chambers, Station Road, Horley, Surrey, RH6 9HW (tel: 01293 774 535).

DRIVING
Car hire
It is possible to take your own car to the islands via mainland Spain, but as the Canary Islands provide very reasonable car hire rates, it hardly seems worth the effort or expense.

Reliable and competitively priced local firms include Top-Car Reisen, with airport offices on Gran Canaria (tel: 57 47 44), Tenerife South/Reina Sofia (tel: 77 32 06), Tenerife North/Los Rodeos (tel: 26 22 02) and facilities at Lanzarote (tel: 57 47 44). Alternatively, if you wish to book from the UK, Europe's largest car-hire brokers, Holiday Autos, 25 Sackville Road, London W1X 1AA, have a lowest-price guarantee (tel: 0171 491 1111).

Documentation
All British, European, American and Australian driving licences are valid though it may be advisable to take a Spanish translation with you (contact a motoring organisation in your own country before travelling). An International Driving Permit is not necessary.

Petrol
Petrol is expensive and it's best to carry cash, as the majority of petrol stations do not accept credit cards. These are relatively numerous along the main roads with 24-hour opening in the larger resorts and towns. Don't drive into the mountains on an empty tank however. There are few, if any, filling stations and those steep winding roads are very thirsty.

Beware of goats on Fuerteventura!

Gran Canaria's road signs are works of art

Rules of the road

Driving is on the right. Seat belts are compulsory. Children under 10 must travel in the back of the car. In towns cars must be parked facing the direction of the movement of traffic. The standard of roads is surprisingly high, with many newly built and very smoothly surfaced. Motorways (*autopista*) run along the north and east coast of Tenerife and the east coast of Gran Canaria, connecting airports with major resorts in 30 minutes or less.

The standard of driving is quite reasonable, though do beware of oncoming traffic and impatient drivers on hairpin bends in mountainous areas.

Beware of traffic jams in Las Palmas, Puerto de la Cruz and Santa Cruz (Gran Canaria) and (Tenerife). Parking is also very difficult in these towns. Las Palmas is particularly bad, though it is sometimes possible to park on the front at Santa Cruz. Beware the fiendish one-way systems in Las Palmas, Puerto de la Cruz and Arrecife on Lanzarote.

ELECTRICITY

The current throughout the islands is 220 volts AC and sockets take the circular two-pin continental-style plug. If you are really out in the wilds you may find 110 volts supply, but this is rare. Ask if in doubt.

Power cuts are not infrequent, so pack a torch.

EMBASSIES AND CONSULATES

The following addresses are all consulates. Embassies are located in Madrid.

Ireland Calle Castillo 8, Santa Cruz, Tenerife (tel: 24 56 71).
UK Plaza de Weyler 8, Santa Cruz, Tenerife (tel: 28 68 63).
Edificio Cataluña, Calle de Luis Morote, 6, 35007, Las Palmas, Gran Canaria (tel: 26 25 08/12/16).
USA Calle Franchy Roca, 5, Las Palmas, Gran Canaria (tel: 27 12 59).

EMERGENCY TELEPHONE NUMBERS

Police (all islands): 091

Province of Tenerife

Red Cross (Cruz Roja): all islands 28 29 24
Ambulance: Tenerife – Santa Cruz 28 18 00; Puerto de la Cruz, 38 38 12; Los Cristianos 79 05 05; Playa de las Américas 71 06 20.
Fire: Santa Cruz, Tenerife 22 00 80; Puerto de la Cruz, Tenerife 33 00 80; Tenerife South 73 22 80; La Palma 41 11 50

Province of Gran Canaria

Red Cross (Cruz Roja): all islands 23 00 00.
Ambulance: all islands 24 59 21.
Fire: Gran Canaria 20 71 22; Lanzarote 81 01 11 or 81 06 11 or 81 48 58.

The cool green foliage of a city park provides shelter from the heat and hassle of the streets

HEALTH

No vaccinations are necessary for a visit to the Canary Islands. EU citizens can obtain a refund of most medical costs by using form E111 (available from post offices and Health and/or Social Security offices in your own country). If you don't take this along, you can still claim back later (remember to keep all receipts). Medical insurance is still strongly advisable.

The most common complaints are stomach upsets caused by a sudden change of diet and too much sun. Break yourself in gradually to sunbathing and always use suntan lotions and blocks. Remember that children are particularly vulnerable.

There are many English-speaking dentists and doctors throughout the islands. Ask your hotel or tourist information office for the nearest one. Minor ailments can usually be treated at the chemist (*farmacia*). At least one chemist per town or area stays open after hours. Its location is posted in the window of all the other chemists (also available from the tourist office and local newspaper).

HITCH-HIKING

This is legal, though not commonly practised, and with the large number of North European holiday drivers on the roads, not likely to be a quick way of getting around. An official hitch-hiker's card (obtainable from Youth Hostel Associations) may help.

It is unwise to hitch alone.

LANGUAGE

Canary Islanders speak Spanish, or to be more accurate Castilian (the language of most of mainland Spain). The only real difference that the non-language student will notice is that the letter **c** and **z** are pronounced (softly), instead of lisped with a 'th' sound.

There are a few indigenous words still in use, the most notable being **papa(s)** for potato(es) and **guagua** (pronounced wah-wah) for bus.

It's quite possible in some major resorts to get through two weeks on the islands speaking, and even hearing, nothing other than English. However, off the beaten track, and particularly on the smaller islands a smattering of Spanish will be helpful if not essential. But wherever you are, your attempts to master a few phrases and, at the very least, daily greetings will always be appreciated.

Pronunciation

Try to remember the following basic rules:
Vowels:

a is a short 'ah' sound – **gracias** (thank you). It is never long as in the English 'gracious'. All the other vowels are long sounds. The letter **e** is a cross between the short English e (as in get) and the long English a (as in grace) – **de** (of/from) is pronounced 'day' but in a clipped way. The letter **i** is a long 'ee' sound as in **sí** (yes), pronounced 'see', and **u** is like 'oo' in boot – **una** (one).

Consonants:

c is soft before e and i (e.g. Barcelona) but hard at any other time – **como?** (pardon?) pronounced 'ko-mo'.

g at the start of a word is a hard sound (as in get). In the middle of a word it is like the throaty 'ch' as in the Scottish 'loch' – **urgencia** (emergency) is pronounced 'ooer-chensee-ah'. In **agua** (water) it is hardly pronounced at all ('ah-kwa').

h is always silent – **hospital** is pronounced 'ospitahl'.

j is also pronounced like the ch in 'loch' – **jamón** (ham) is pronounced 'ch-amon'.

ll is always like 'll' in million – **lleno** (full) is prononunced 'lyay-no'.

ñ is like 'ni' in onion – **España** (Spain) is pronounced 'ay-spanya'.

qu is like k in key – **quanto?** (how much?) is pronounced 'kwan-toe'.

r is rolled: **rr** is rolled even harder.

v is like b in bottle – **vino** (wine) is pronounced 'bee-no'.

x is like s – **excelente** (excellent) is pronounced 'ess-say-len-tay'.

Numbers

0	**cero**
1	**uno/a**
2	**dos**
3	**tres**
4	**cuatro**
5	**cinco**
6	**seis**
7	**siete**
8	**ocho**
9	**nueve**

10	**diez**	good morning	**buenos días**
11	**once**	good afternoon	**buenas tardes**
12	**doce**	goodnight	**buenas noches**
13	**trece**	goodbye	**adiós**
14	**catorce**	please	**por favor**
15	**quince**	thank you	**gracias**
16	**dieciséis**	you're welcome	**de nada**
17	**diecisiete**	today	**hoy**
18	**dieciocho**	tomorrow	**mañana**
19	**diecinueve**	yesterday	**ayer**
20	**veinte**	I am English	**Soy inglés**
21	**veintiuno**	do you speak	
30	**treinta**	English?	**¿habla inglés?**
40	**cuarenta**		(informal)
50	**cincuenta**		**¿habla usted**
60	**sesenta**		**inglés?** (formal)
70	**setenta**	very well/good	**muy bien/vale**
80	**ochenta**	where is ...?	**¿dónde está...?**
90	**noventa**	what/when	**qué/cuándo**
100	**cien/ciento**	why/how	**por qué/cómo**
101	**ciento uno/a**	how much is...?	**¿cuánto**
200	**doscientos/as**		**vale/cuesta...?**
500	**quinientos/as**	here/there	**aquí/ahí**
1000	**mil**	open/closed	**abierto/cerrado**
2000	**dos mil**	right, left	**derecho/a,**
1,000,000	**un millón**		**izquierdo/a**
		sorry!	**¡lo siento!**

Days of the week

		excuse me	
Sunday	**domingo**	(can I get past?)	**perdóneme**
Monday	**lunes**	(can you help?)	**por favor –**
Tuesday	**martes**	(sir, madam,	**señor, señora,**
Wednesday	**miércoles**	miss)	**señorita**
Thursday	**jueves**	I don't	**no**
Friday	**viernes**	understand	**comprendo**
Saturday	**sábado**	I would like...	**quiero/quisiera...**
		large/small	**grande/pequeño**

Useful words and phrases

yes/no	**sí/no**	do you have...?	**¿tiene...?**
hello	**hola**	please write	**por favor,**
		it down	**escríbalo**

LAUNDRY

All hotels of a reasonable size will provide a laundry service, albeit at a price that makes hand-washing an attractive alternative. You will find a self-service launderette (*lavandería*) in each major resort and town.

LOST PROPERTY

Lost property offices are few and far between. Ask the tourist office where to go locally. Report lost valuables to the Municipal Police or *Guardia Civil* and obtain a form for your own holiday insurance purposes.

MAPS

As new roads continue to be built so maps go out of date quite rapidly. The *AA Macmillan Canary Islands* map is recommended. Town plans and basic local maps are usually available from tourist offices.

MEDIA

There are several newspapers and magazines written for the English-speaking visitor to the Canary Islands. Gran Canaria has surprisingly little. Lanzarote has *Lanzarote Holiday Gazette* (free) and *Lancelot*, available from newsagents. On Tenerife look out for the newspaper *Island Connections* and the monthly magazine *Island Gazette* in the newsagents plus the free magazine *Tenerife Holiday Gazette*. La Palma has an annual magazine guide, *Guía Practica*.

Free magazines are generally available from tourist offices, travel agents, hotels and popular bars.

All the major international papers are available in the large towns and popular resorts the day after publication, though the *International Herald Tribune* and *The Guardian* (international edition) can

arrive the same day.

Radio Canarias-Sol provides news and tourist information in English (Monday to Friday 8–8.30am, 3–3.30pm, 4.30–5pm) and German at most other times on 99.6 FM. Radio Maspalomas also provides a German language magazine programme from Sunday to Friday 6–8pm from Sunday to Friday on 95.3 FM.

On Tenerife Canary Island Tourist Radio broadcasts in English from Monday to Saturday on 747 MW.

MONEY MATTERS

The *peseta* (pta) is the Spanish unit of currency used throughout the islands. There are banknotes for 1,000, 2,000, 5,000 and 10,000 pesetas and coins in denominations of 1, 5, 10, 25, 50, 100, 200 and 500 pesetas. There is no limit to the amount of money you may bring onto the islands but you cannot take out more than 500,000 pesetas.

Banks are open on weekdays from 9am to 2pm and from 9am to 1pm on Saturdays (closed on Saturdays from 1 June to 31 October). A commission is always charged for changing money (often hefty, so exchange large amounts if possible) and you will need your passport. Outside banking hours many travel agents and various *bureaux de change* (look for the *cambio* sign) will exchange money, but always at a lower rate than the bank. Even if the rates on display seem attractive, the deductions which they fail to advertise will cost you dearly (tourist shops are the worst culprits in this respect). Most hotels will also change money.

OPENING HOURS

Shops are open Monday to Saturday, 9am–1pm and 4 or 5pm to 7 or 8pm

The Catholic church of Inglesia San Francisco, Santa Cruz de Tenerife

(chemists usually close on Saturday afternoon). Aside from major tourist resorts, shops are closed on Sunday. Museum opening hours are variable; some close on Sunday, others on a Monday (or another weekday), while some remain open all week. Church hours are also unpredictable. Morning or evening services are usually the best times to find them open.

PLACES OF WORSHIP

Catholic mass is celebrated in various languages in all the major resorts throughout the Canary Islands. Ask the tourist office, see the local newspapers, · or look on church notice boards for details.

There are Anglican churches at Ciudad Jardin, Las Palmas (Calle Brasil/Rafael Ramirez) on Gran Canaria; Nuestra Señora de Carmen church at the old town harbour, Puerto del Carmen on Lanzarote. On Tenerife Protestant services are held in the Anglican church at Taoro Park, Puerto de la Cruz, the church on the Plaza de los Patos in Santa Cruz, the Casa Sueca in Los Cristianos and in the Pueblo Canario in Playa de las Américas.

The Ecumenical Church in Playa del Inglés (Gran Canaria) is used by several denominations. There is a synagogue in Calle Remedios, Las Palmas.

Evangelical services take place on Tenerife at Hotel Andreas, Los Cristianos and the Evangelical Church on Calle Iriarte, Puerto de la Cruz.

POLICE

Police responsibilities are split three ways on the islands. The *Policía Municipal* (blue uniform and cap) direct traffic and have other municipal duties; the *Policía Nacional* (brown uniform and beret) are in charge of crime in the towns; the *Guardia Civil* (pea-green uniform and cap) look after crime and patrol the highways in rural areas.

POSTAL SERVICES

Post offices are open weekdays 9am to 2pm and 9am to 1pm on Saturday. There are no telephones in post offices but you can send a telegram from larger branches, or dictate one by telephone: 22 20 00.

Stamps (*sellos* or *timbres*) can also be bought at tobacconists and most shops which sell postcards.

Postboxes are painted yellow. Use the slot marked *extranjeros* (foreign) for postcards home.

PUBLIC HOLIDAYS

1 January New Year's Day
6 January Epiphany
2 February Candlemas
19 March St Joseph's Day
1 May Labour Day
25 July St James's Day
15 August Assumption
12 October Columbus Day
1 November All Saints' Day
6 December Constitution Day
8 December Immaculate Conception
25 December Christmas Day

Moveable feasts are Maundy Thursday, Good Friday, Corpus Christi, and Conception (usually 8 December). In addition to these, there are several local feast days.

PUBLIC TRANSPORT
Air

Binter airlines, a subsidiary of the national airline, Iberia (tel: London 0171 830 0011), runs regular flights between all the islands (the airport on La Gomera is currently under construction). These are punctual and all flights are around 30 minutes. Enquire at any airport for a timetable or contact the local Binter offices at: Los Rodeos on Tenerife (tel:

The 'Won't-take-no-for-an-answer' attitude of some time-share touts can be frustrating

23 43 46, 23 48 22 or 26 01 01); La
Palma (tel: 41 15 40).

Ferries

Ferries run to all the islands and
hydrofoils or jetfoils run between
Tenerife and La Gomera; Gran Canaria
and Tenerife; and between both Tenerife
and Gran Canaria to Fuerteventura. The
main ferry operator is **Compañía
Trasmediterránea**, who have offices on
the islands all except El Hierro:
Arrecife, Lanzarote (tel: 81 11 88)
Las Palmas, Gran Canaria (tel: 26 77
66)
Puerto del Rosario, Fuerteventura (tel:
85 08 77)
Santa Cruz, Tenerife (tel: 28 78 50)
Santa Cruz, La Palma (tel: 41 16 06)
San Sebastián, La Gomera (tel: 87 13 24)
The Trasmediterránea agent in Britain is
Southern Ferries, 179 Piccadilly,
London W1V 9DB (tel: 0171 491 4968).
   Other ferry companies are:
Betancuria (Lanzarote–Fuerteventura
service). Offices in Arrecife, Lanzarote
(tel: 81 25 34) and Corralejo,
Fuerteventura (tel: 41 72 14 or 51 72
66).
Ferry Gomera (Tenerife–Gomera
service). Offices in Los Cristianos,
Tenerife (tel: 79 05 56) and San
Sebastián, La Gomera (tel: 87 10 07).
Fred Olsen (Lanzarote–Fuerteventura).
Offices in Playa Blanca, Lanzarote (tel:
51 72 66) and Corralejo, Fuerteventura.

Buses

The bus service (buses are known as
guaguas) on Gran Canaria and Tenerife,
run by TITSA, is fast and reliable. The
smaller islands are less well served. If you
intend travelling a lot on buses, consider
a *bono* (literally, voucher) which for a
reasonable annual amount entitles you to

buy tickets at 40 per cent discount
(available from main bus stations).
Central bus station telephone numbers
are as follows:
Gran Canaria 36 10 79
La Gomera 21 90 33, 21 92 44, 21 90 55
or 21 90 99
La Palma 41 19 24, 41 44 41 or 42 00
60
Tenerife, Playa de Las Américas 79 54
27 and Puerto de la Cruz 38 18 07
Fuerteventura 85 09 51
Lanzarote 81 15 46 or 81 24 58

Taxis

These are recognisable by a green light in
the windscreen or on a white roof and an
official plate with the letters SP, standing
for *servicio público* (public service). The
light shows *libre* (free) when they are
available for hire. For short trips within
tourist areas many cabbies won't bother
to put their meters on, though you will
rarely be cheated. Boards by the main
taxi ranks display fixed prices between
the most popular destinations.
   A cab here is still good value by north
European standards. For longer
distances however confirm the price, or
rate, before you start.

SENIOR CITIZENS

Senior citizens are well catered for by
many hotels on Gran Canaria, Tenerife,
and to a lesser extent, Lanzarote, by
specific styles of holidays and long-stay
discounts.

STUDENT AND YOUTH TRAVEL

For various reasons the Canary Islands
do not attract the back-packing
youngsters seen in many other holiday
islands throughout the world. There are
very few official camping sites and no
youth hostels.

Calling home has never been easier

Telefónicas are generally in central locations and open late. Hotels usually levy a hefty surcharge. Calls are cheaper after 10pm.

For international calls, dial 07, wait for the tone to indicate that you have a line, then dial your country code (Australia 61, Canada and the USA 1, Ireland 353, UK 44), followed by the local code (omitting the first 0), then the number.

Each Canary province has its own code: 928 for Gran Canaria, Lanzarote and Fuerteventura, 922 for Tenerife, La Gomera, El Hierro and La Palma. When you are calling from outside the Canaries, drop the 9.

TIME

The Canaries maintain Greenwich Mean Time in the winter, which is one hour behind most European countries and in line with the UK. The clocks go back one hour in summer.

The Canaries are five hours ahead of US Eastern Standard Time, and eight hours ahead of Pacific Time. Johannesburg is ahead by one hour, Australia by 10 hours and New Zealand by 12 hours.

Note that there are two brief periods of a one-hour difference (in late September and late March) owing to different start/end dates to summer.

TIPPING

Most hotels and some restaurant bills include a service charge. A small tip (around 10 per cent) for a well-served meal, a friendly taxi driver, or hotel staff who have been particularly helpful, will be appreciated. Don't forget to leave the hotel maid something, too.

TELEPHONES

You can now make international calls from virtually any phone on the islands. The best way to phone home is from a *telefónica* cabin, which comprises metered booths where you pay after your call. This is not much more expensive than a street phone and is much less draughty, less noisy and you don't need mountains of change to hand. The LED indicator above your phone is *not* the amount in pesetas you are spending, but the unit charge (which is considerably less).

TOILETS

Public toilets are very rare and recommendable public toilets rarer still. In order of preference, use those in hotels, restaurants and bars. Buy a drink in the latter as a matter of courtesy.

There are several terms for toilets: *servicios*, *aseos*, WC, *retretes*. The doors are usually marked *Señoras* (ladies) and *Caballeros* (gentlemen).

TOURIST INFORMATION

All the islands have a central tourist office (*turismo*) and the larger resorts have their own town offices (listed in What to See under the appropriate locations). Free maps and leaflets are usually on offer together with bus timetables (not to be taken away) and sometimes other 'what's on' lists. All offices have at least one English-speaking member of staff but the service you get

Tiles prove their versatility in Santa Cruz de Tenerife

depends very much on which member of staff you see. All offices should be able to help you with accommodation.

Before you leave home write to the Spanish National Tourist Office for information:
United Kingdom: 57–8 St James's Street, London SW1A 1LD (tel: 0171 499 09 01)
USA: 665 Fifth Avenue, New York, NY 10022 (tel: 212 759 88 22)
Canada: 102 Bloor Street West, 14th Floor, Toronto, Ontario M5S 1M8 (tel: 416 961 31 31)
Australia: 203 Castlereagh Street, Level 2–Suite 21a, PO Box 675, 2000 Sydney NSW (tel: 02 264 79 66)

Santa Cruz de Tenerife tile sign

ACKNOWLEDGEMENTS

The Automobile Association wishes to thank the following photographers and libraries for their assistance in the preparation of this book.
J ALLAN CASH PHOTOLIBRARY 150, 151; MARY EVANS/EXPLORER 37; P MURPHY 16, 49, 61, 79, 115, 127, 138a, 142, 146a, 146b, 147a, 147b; PICTURES COLOUR LIBRARY LTD 119, 129a, 129b, 130, 149; SPECTRUM COLOUR LIBRARY 38, 75, 143; THE MANSELL COLLECTION 132; WORLD PICTURES Spine
The remaining photographs are held in the Association's library own library (AA PHOTO LIBRARY) and were taken by Clive Sawyer.

The author wishes to thank the following organisations for their kind hospitality and assistance in the preparation of this guide: Top Car Reisen Car Hire company; Paradores de Turismo de España and Keytel International; Hotel Ifa Faro, Maspalomas; Patronato Insular de Turismo de Gran Canaria. Thanks also to: Holiday Autos Car Hire; Apartamentos Lanzamar (Puerto del Carmen); Caravana Viajes/Whitehall Leisure Travel Agents (Puerto del Carmen).

CONTRIBUTORS
Series adviser: Melissa Shales **Copy editor:** Nia Williams **Verifier:** Jenny Fry **Designer:** Design 23
Indexer: Marie Lorimer